One Person Can Make A Difference

Doris Ross Reddick
One Person Can Make A Difference

Her Story In Her Own Words
As Told To
Ersula K Odom

Sula Too Publishing

Copyright © 2015, 2021 by Doris Ross Reddick

All rights reserved. No part of this book may be reproduced in any form or by any electronic or mechanical means, including information storage and retrieval systems, without permission in writing from the author, except by reviewer or presenter, who may quote brief passages in a review or presentation.

Co-written with Ersula K Odom
Edited by Phyllis Reddick

Other books by Doris Ross Reddick:
"Let's Cross Over the Wall"-
    co-written with Altamese Simmons
"Introduction to Word Processing –
    Using Theology to Teach Technology" -
    co-written with Clemmie Perry

Published by Sula Too Publishing, Tampa Florida
Printed in the United States of America
www.sulatoo.com/publishing

Library of Congress Control Number: 2020952794

Second Edition
ISBN-13: 978-1-7358398-7-5
ISBN-10:   1-7358398-7-5
Ebook   978-1-7358398-8-2
10 9 8 7 6 5 4 3 2

1. African Americans – Florida – Hillsborough County - Tampa

Contents

Dedication	5
Foreword	6
The Making of Doris	7
Family Matters	13
A Family of My Own	47
Education Began at Home	53
Mother/Daughter Love	73
Civil Rights for All	83
A Lifetime of Service	91
A New Beginning	99
Hillsborough County School Board	105
My Spiritual Experience	129
Words That Linger	133
Conclusion - Having a Perpetual Impact	141
Doris Ross Reddick Summary & Reference	143

Doris Ross Reddick

Dedication

I dedicate this book to my lovely children Kenneth, Ross and Clemmie Perry.

As you enter my home, this is what you will see, my family. Yes, I have accomplished a great deal. However, what I want to share, and what this book is about, is the loving support my family provided as I served my community. Therefore, I also dedicate it to my entire family. I love you.

Foreword

One would define a matriarch as an individual who strengthens and serves as the nucleus of the family. Like Doris, matriarchs provide unconditional love, a wealth of knowledge and a level of wisdom that would amaze any icon or renowned person. They know how to be whatever you need them to be at the right time. They keep you warm when you are cold, are your best friend, your cheerleader, or a shoulder to lean on. Most importantly, they unselfishly expose you to invaluable life experiences. My Dearest Doris Ross Reddick is a model matriarch. Our bond is unique. The family often referred to me as Harold and Doris' baby girl. But to me, she has served as a second mother and a special aunt. Doris Ross Reddick is my matriarch and a woman with a rich legacy that will never be forgotten.

Lovingly,
Alva Simmons

The Making of Doris

Doris Ross Reddick

A Little Girl's Dream

My life sprang from the words of a six or seven-year-old girl with a vision. She said, "When I grow up, I'm going to get married, have a little girl, name her Doris and she is going to be a teacher."

My name is Doris, and the little girl was my mother, little Clemmie Simmons.

It is natural to hear a child talk about their "play-play babies" while staring into the eyes of a plastic doll. It was notably uncommon for a child to look adults squarely in the face and predict the future with such conviction. This little girl's dream would ultimately mold countless lives as it materialized.

Young Doris Gwendolyn Ross

Dreams in the Making

Our known ancestral dreams began a decade or two before Abraham Lincoln was elected as the sixteenth president of the United States in 1861. While in office (1861-1865), it became necessary for him to declare a state of insurrection due to the dispute between the North and South over slavery. This insurrection developed into the American Civil War and could have destroyed the nation. To save the Union, in September 1862, President Lincoln issued the Emancipation Proclamation, a document which freed the slaves. It became effective in January 1863. However, the American Civil War actually ended in April 1865 at Appomattox, Virginia, when Robert E. Lee, the Confederate general, surrendered to Ulysses S. Grant, a Union general.

Prior to these events, some place on the southeastern shores of the American continent, Paul Sloan met and married Harriett and became the stepfather of her young son Jim Sherman. Jim, born in North Carolina, was said to have been fathered by one of Harriet's white master's sons, a member of the Wilkerson family.

In the years that followed, the couple became parents of many other children. In addition to Jim, the children reaching adulthood were Willie Ben, Alfred, George, Andrew, Johnny, Paul Jr, Charlie, Matilda, and Anita.

Paul, Harriett, and their young son Jim were the legal property of the Mays Family of Madison County, founded by Rev. Richard Johnson Mays. It is believed that the Mays Family also owned some of Paul and Harriett's other children as well as Jim. They brought Paul, Harriett, and family to Jefferson and Madison counties. The Mays family, who were planters, owned a large plantation. The section where slaves and later free persons lived was called Mays Island or Mays Landing. This area was not an island by definition, but a part of the land set aside for black inhabitants. Because of limited written records and little oral history, it is not clearly understood how or exactly when Paul, Harriett, and little Jim were brought to the settlement.

During a parallel time in history, Joseph King and Susan became man and wife. They were also owned by the Mays family and lived on Mays Island near Harriett and Paul Sloan. As was the custom of the times, Joseph and Susan gave birth to many children. Their children who survived to adulthood were: Ezekiel, Dora, Ann, Clara, Amanda, Nathaniel, Steve, Eliza, William, Susan, Collie, Brack, Sophia, Adaline, and Julia. It is unknown how, when or with whom Joseph and Susan arrived on Mays Island. The Sloan family came from South Carolina.

When slaves eventually gained their freedom, Jim Sherman married Jane Wright, a daughter of Josh and Sylvia Wright. Jane, a member of the King family, was born in South Carolina. However, now she was among the clan belonging to and living on the Mays family estate. As a young child during winter nights, one of Jane's duties was to serve as a foot warmer for the ladies in the big house. Yes, she had to sleep at the foot of the bed to keep their feet warm

Several young Sloan men married several of the young ladies from the King family, thus connecting the Sloan-King families at multiple points. To these young people, a third generation was born. After the Emancipation Proclamation, the Kings, Sloan and Jim Sherman (as others) were considered freedmen and women. Many of them decided to remain in Madison, Florida, the home of their Florida ancestors. Other family members chose to leave and make new homes for themselves in various parts of the state and nation. Today the Sloan and King descendants are worldwide.

As for Jim Sherman, my biracial great grandfather, we are uncertain of the origin of the name Sherman. However, since his time, we have claimed it as our own.

Family Tree

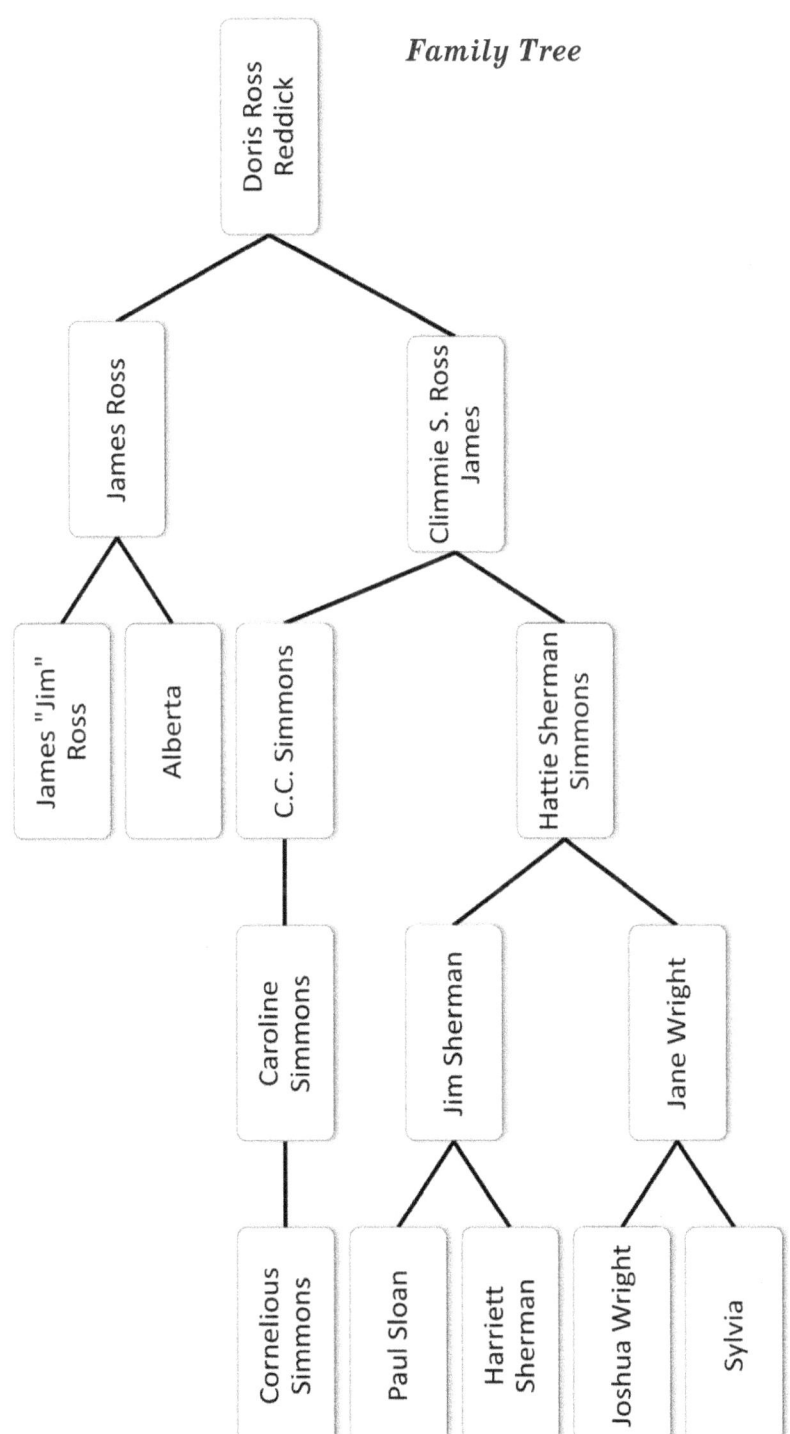

Christmas 1960 - 4 Generations of Simmons Family: Hattie "Mother Hattie" Simmons, Ross A. Perry, Clemmie C. "Baby Clemmie" Perry, Clemmie "Granny" James. Doris "Mom" Perry & Kenneth C. Perry.

One Person Can Make A Difference

Family Matters

Jim & Clemmie Ross

James Ross

Clemmie Simmons Ross

Doris Ross

Doris Ross Reddick

Jim Ross

James Ross was born into a farming family in Sycamore, near Fort Valley, Georgia. He moved to the city because he wanted to become a barber and he did. Young James heard about the Pullman Porters and that the money was good. He became a Pullman Porter was one of the most illustrious jobs a black person could have at the time.

He met and married Clemmie Simmons, who was born in Quitman Georgia, the daughter of a preacher and housewife. Clemmie and James met and were married. They purchased a little house before I was born, but they didn't live in it due to his extensive Pullman travels. Instead, Mother went to her mother's home for me to be born and never returned to the house. My parents divorced, the day after father remarried, he died. For the short time, my father and I shared this earth together, he loved me dearly and always came home bearing gifts for me.

One Person Can Make A Difference

C. C. & Hattie Simmons - Mother's Parents

Rev. Christopher Columbus Simmons

Hattie Sherman Simmons

Rev. C.C. Simmons and Hattie Sherman Simmons were my maternal grandparents. I find it amusing that my grandfather's name really was Christopher Columbus Simmons. Mother Hattie told me stories about their life experiences. My grandfather, Rev C.C. Simmons, was an A.M.E. Church minister who pastored several churches in Florida in Jacksonville, Daytona, Lake City and Palatka.

Three of their children, Eva, Elsie, and Leola, were enrolled in Mrs. Bethune's Boarding School, Daytona Industrial School for Girls. My grandfather and grandmother became friends of Mrs. Bethune and supported the school. They were also involved in civil rights efforts with her.

Doris Ross Reddick

When Mother Hattie needed surgery and was hospitalized, Mrs. Bethune walked beside the gurney as they were wheeling her into surgery, singing "Leaning on the Everlasting Arms" (B-CC's shibboleth and watch word).

Rev. C. C. Simmons

In Jacksonville on October 15, 1989, a portrait of Rev. Simmons was presented to Mount Moriah A.M.E. by his grandchildren with the following inscription:

> Rev. C. C. Simmons, D.D.
> Edward Waters College Graduate
> Pastor, Mount Moriah A.M.E. Church 1912-1915
> Bishop John Hurst, Presiding Prelate
> A Tribute for Continuing Worship and Service, in the Christian Tradition.
> Presented by descendants of Rev. C.C. Simmons
> October 15, 1989
> Rev. Dr. Calvin S. McFarland, Sr., Pastor

The grandchildren shared the expense to present a portrait and a cash donation to the church. Grandchildren attending were: Doris, Al, and Patrick, and great-grandchild, Ken.

Pastor McFarland shared his research and interviews with us. His interviews of the older members of their community provided valuable details about Grandfather. C.C. Simmons. He was described as extremely handsome, tall, a stately, classy gentleman with very fine skin. They said his mannerisms matched his ministerial responsibilities. Pastor McFarland also shared that during Rev. Simmons' tenure as pastor of the church, he was responsible for the construction of the sanctuary from the basement up. For that reason, his name was placed on the cornerstone where the addition to the church was constructed.

Grandfather was also pastor of St. Stephen A.M.E. and Greater Grant Memorial A.M.E. Churches, both in Jacksonville, Florida. I was so excited when I found my grandfather's name listed on the internet as a part of the Grant Memorial A.M.E.'s history. Records state that Reverend C.C. Simmons was there from the beginning and served as its third pastor.

Jim and Jane Sherman
Grandmother Hattie's Parents
(my great grands)

Jim Sherman

Jane Sherman

Uncommon Bonds

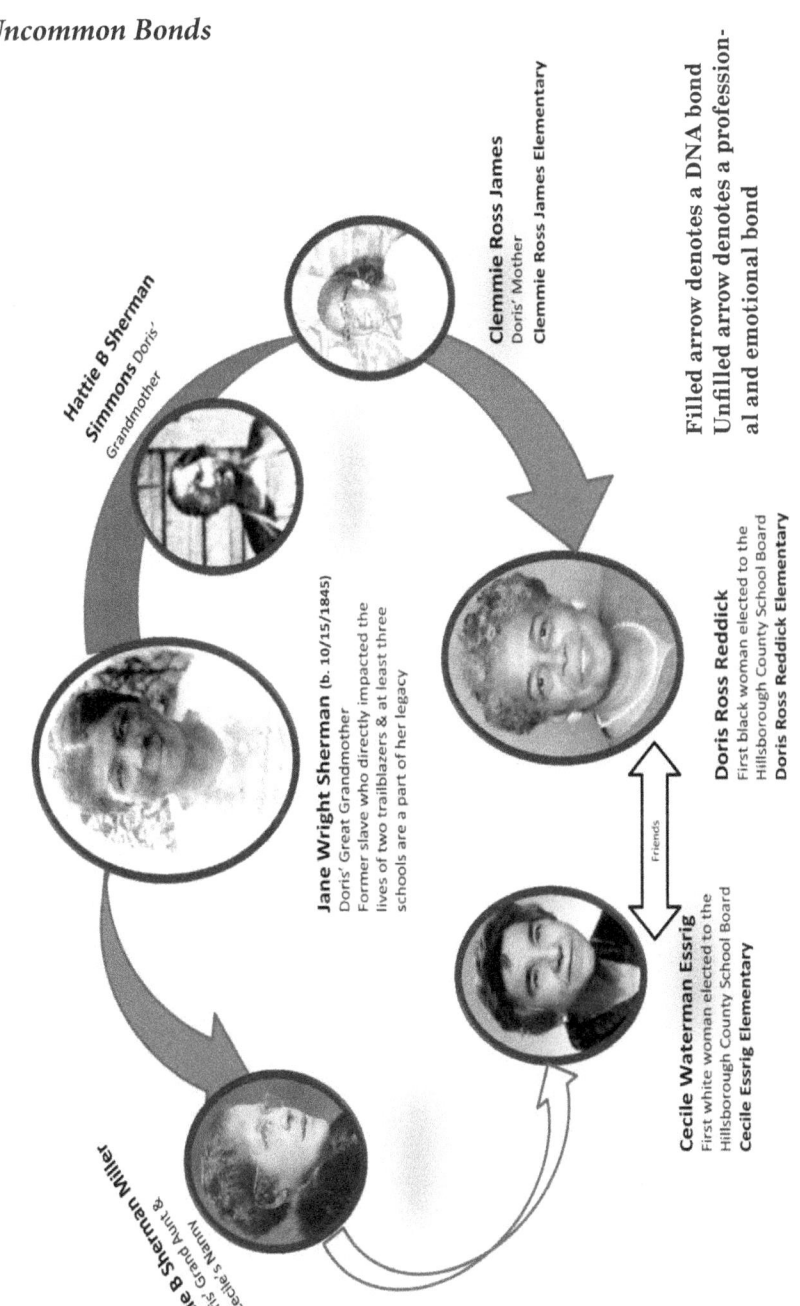

The union of my great-grandparents, Jim and Jane Sherman began a legacy that is felt, at least nationwide, because of the daily nurturing Jane provided. "Uncommon Bonds" highlights her story and how one person's impact can span generations. The bonds that were created are extraordinary.

Jane Sherman, my maternal great-grandmother, was a former slave who had several children, two of whom are featured in this story. Jane's daughter, Pattie B. Sherman Miller, was hired by Daisy Waterman to care for her daughter, Cecile Waterman. Jane's daughter, Hattie B. Sherman Simmons, was the mother of Clemmie Simmons Ross and the grandmother of Doris Ross. Cecile Waterman Essrig became the first white woman elected to Hillsborough County School Board. I, Doris Ross Reddick, became the first black woman elected to the Hillsborough County School Board. Cecile and I were friends. There are schools named for Cecile, Clemmie and me, Cecile Essrig Elementary, Clemmie Ross James Educational Center, and Doris Ross Reddick Elementary.

My grandmother Hattie was a nanny for Attorney K.I. McKay's children from the D.B. McKay Family. At my 80th birthday party, I asked my friend, Shirley McKay, Attorney K.I. McKay's daughter, "Shirley, what did Grandmother Hattie and you talk about?" Shirley's answer to the audience was, "The same thing she talked about with you, Doris." Shirley and I were the apples of Hattie's eye. She told Shirley stories about me and vice versa. We ran parallel lives as Shirley was only one year younger than me. When I heard of her death in 2014, a chapter in my life closed.

Mother, Clemmie Simmons Ross James, served 70 years in the Hillsborough County School system in many professional capacities, from teacher, to assistant principal, to you name it she did it.

So, Jane Sherman, a former slave provided nurturing, moral support, companionship, love, and guidance that led to at least two women making Hillsborough County history and schools being named for three people her loving ways impacted.

The "Uncommon Bond" spanned another generation on February 21, 2013, when Cecile Waterman Essrig's daughters and I had a two-hour, highly interactive lunch. Suitable for the magnitude of the occasion, we dined in downtown Tampa's historic and beautifully renovated Floridian Hotel. "Look up", said Lee, pointing to the marvelous ceiling, and the glory of the day began. The memories of Cecile Essrig, Jane Sherman, Pattie Bell Sherman Miller, and Hattie Bertenia Sherman Simmons danced around the room. It is amazing how a hotel that once advertised their "all white" experience (including staff) was now host to such a historic and loving meeting.

The Essrig sisters, Lee and Katherine, recalled their mother Cecile's unpretentious, caring and soft-spoken strength, and my aunt Pattie's elegance, and her love for children. They acknowledged the totally compatible souls of these women in life and in death.

I told them how determined Jane Sherman had been for her children to go to school, rain or shine. In turn, Katherine talked about how she typed countless speeches and invocations from her mother's dictation. Described by Lee, Cecile Essrig's compassion for people was tangible.

The sisters left on a mission to return to their mother's "red box" in search of hidden memories. Even though they were both lawyers, one a judge and the other a quality assurance specialist, the childlike joy of realizing that their mother's memory lives on in all of us, appeared liberating.

Katherine Essrig, Doris Ross Reddick, C. Lee Essrig after lunch at The Floridian Hotel

During Aunt Pattie's last days, Cecile accompanied me to The Robert City Hotel to see her one last time. Aunt Pattie co-owned The Roberts City Hotel with her daughter, Eloise Miller Jones.

It was a profound honor to grow up with my great grandmother. She shared her experiences and desires for her children with all her descendants. Her words of belief, faith, trust, self-reliance, and confidence carried me from a two-story white house on a sand filled street in West Tampa away from the cook stove in Hyde Park; away from the wash tubs full of clothes that were not mine; away from attending to babies that were not mine at night. Her words and love carried me from birth to Bethune-Cookman College, through the University of South Florida to the chair of the Hillsborough County School Board, a place where no other black woman had ever been.

1335 Green Street

I was born on 1335 Green Street in my Grandmother Hattie's house that was affectionately known as "the family home". Several of my cousins were born there as well. The maternal nurturing at 1335 Green Street spanned multiple generations. At times, there were four generations in one home. For that reason, it is necessary for me to illustrate who my "mothers" were.

"Grand"
Jane Sherman

"Mother Hattie"
Hattie B. Simmons

"Mother"
Clemmie James

"Me"
Doris R. Reddick

1335 Green Street – Mother Hattie Standing and Clemmie James Sitting

"Mother Hattie" was an African Methodist Episcopal (A.M.E.) pastor's wife and the family moved from place to place as he ministered to assigned congregations. Unfortunately, my grandfather died young leaving Mother Hattie alone with six children; Clemmie, Ethel, Eva, Leola, Hattie, and Alphonso.

One night shortly after her husband died, Mother Hattie said, "the spirit" visited her while she slept and told her to move to Tampa because that's where she could raise her family. Since her sisters and brothers were in Tampa, she arose and began taking action. She immediately awakened Clemmie, my mother, and explained the plan. "Move to Tampa? Why do we have to move to Tampa?" Mother asked. Then she remembered what happened when her father died in Palatka Florida. Grandfather C.C. Simmons knew he was dying and asked each of his children what kind of father he had been to them. He also gave them instructions on what he expected of each of them. He said to my mother, "Clemmie, you are the oldest and very smart. Your mother is a lovely woman, but she is not up on everything and you will have to help her." As instructed by her father, my mother did just that almost her entire life. Mother Hattie lived a long and happy life, almost as long as my mother. Mother had some help keeping her promise because "the family" was very attentive to Mother Hattie. Therefore, Tampa is where they moved.

Mother Hattie bought a small house in West Tampa. My older cousin, Aunt Eva's son Herbert "Buddy" Butler, holds the honor of being the first grandchild to be born at 1335 Green Street. Because Buddy and I were virtually raised together, I often called him my brother. Aunt Eva owned a small "sundry" store on the corner of Laurel and Willow streets.

Mother Hattie had two grandsons named Herbert. Her youngest child, Hattie B. Curry, passed away when her son Herbert was only eighteen months old. He was raised by his doting father, Herbert Curry Senior, and his father's mother Ida. Herbert Curry Senior never remarried.

"Buddy", Herbert Butler, was less than nine days old when he took his first trip outside which was not an option the house was burning down.

Three of Mother Hattie's grandchildren. Aunt Hattie B's son Herbert G. Curry (an appraiser in Washington DC), and Uncle Jack's children Alphonso Simmons Jr (a State of FL Probation Officer), and Jacquelyn Simmons (died young of Leukemia) – Circa 1942

Unfortunately, the lady next door was outside talking and forgot she had left a piece of wood, which was too long, in her wood burning stove. As part of the wood burned and turned to ash, the weight of the unburned part caused it to drop and ignite the floor. The neighbor's house and my grandmother's house burned down to the ground. All my grandfather's books and materials were lost.

At that time, Mother Hattie was working in Hyde Park, the aristocratic side of town (where the rich white people lived), as a nurse to Attorney K.I. McKay's children. Attorney McKay was a member of the renowned D.B. McKay family. Donald Brenham McKay served as mayor of Tampa for a total of 14 years (1910-1920, 1927-1931).

It was around noon when Mother Hattie learned her house was on fire. Mrs. Olive McKay drove her home. She was not totally shocked because she had dreamed this fire would happen. Once again, a dream prepared her to handle a tragic loss.

Mother Hattie built a new house, where I was born, married to Charles Perry, and where we lived as Mr. & Mrs. Perry for a short while before moving to Grace Street, where I still live.

Buddy's nickname reminds me of how Uncle Jack got his name. Uncle Jack, Mother's brother, was born Alphonso Simmons, named after a king of Spain. When he was about two or three years old, dressed in a new suit, he simply could not contain his excitement. In the middle of his father's sermon he announced, "I'm Little Jack Johnson in a new red suit." He was known as Jack from that day until he died. The real Jack Johnson was John Arthur "Jack" Johnson (March 31, 1878 – June 10, 1946), a famous black boxer. It is the name Uncle Jack used when he played piano for the "Florida Collegians with Little Genevieve". The group often practiced at 1335 Green Street. Uncle Jack, Aunt Eva and Aunt Leola migrated to New York City and made it their home during the 1930s. They were part of the great migration north and were there during the Harlem Renaissance.

Aunt Leola almost took me out of this world when I was about five years old. She and her husband Lymus Richard Wheeler had a big four-door Buick, which they loved dearly. They also loved to go "for a ride" in that car. According to Julia Allen, our neighbor and store owner next door, Aunt Leola was taking us for a ride. Ms. Allen said my dramatic Aunt Leola was angry about something and in a hurry to get going. She was known to say things like "Only God can make a tree." The meaning behind this statement, to the person it was directed, was that he or she was not God and she could do whatever she wanted. She cranked up the car and started driving without realizing that I had gone around the front of the car to get in while the other children had gone behind the car. The car knocked me down and rolled over my leg. Everybody started screaming and someone went into the house yelling to my mother, "Leola just ran over Doris!" Mother had a "conniption" (whatever that meant) and ran in the opposite direction so afraid of what must have happened to her precious baby girl. Since the street was dry sand, my little leg sank down into the sand and I was not hurt.

When Mother received the news that Great Grandmother Jane had died, I was with her at Lomax Elementary School. The principal brought us home.

Mother was seriously afraid of dead people, but she wanted to touch her grandmother. Seeking help from a neighbor Mother said to her, "You put your hand on her face, put my hand on top of yours and then slide your hand out." That's what they did and Mother survived.

When planning the service, Mother Hattie did not want the traditional "wake in the house" the night before the funeral, which angered her sisters especially Aunt Pattie. Mother Hattie compromised and allowed Grand's body in the house the morning before the funeral for a short visitation. My cousins and I all were afraid to come in the house and I shook all night. When morning finally arrived, I stayed in the back and had no idea how many people came to pay their last respects to Grand.

As an adult and new mother, I took my first and second newborn babies to 1335 Green Street during their first week or two of life. I relied on Mother Hattie to know exactly what to do to help me with my babies. By the time our third baby, Clemmie, arrived, I knew how to handle a baby and brought her home to Grace Street. We brought baby Clemmie home wearing a little white dress and placed her in a little white bassinet in the room with us.

When the announcements for newborn white babies were listed in the paper, white babies were referred to as a boy or girl from a certain family. When announcements for newborn black babies were made, it was printed on the Negro Page that x number of Negro females and x number of Negro males were born. This was all too similar to how you report the birth of livestock for me. To this day, I don't like being called a female. I went to the paper for an archived copy of an announcement I missed and was told the paper didn't keep the Negro section of the paper. I still get emotional about that.

Everyone was very upset when the Department of Transportation came through and took our "1335 Green Street family home" away. It was a very pretty house and we had begun to upgrade it with modern appliances of the time. Even though I was my mother's only child, I never felt like one because of 1335 Green Street. To save something of the beloved homestead, Mother brought the fig tree from the yard to Grace Street, which is now on the east side of the house (as shown with me in 2011).

The Green Street fig tree now on Grace Street, 2011

School Days

When my mother passed the Hillsborough County Teacher's Examination, Blanche Armwood who was in charge of "Negro schools," was very pleased. She said to Mother, "Oh, we are so glad to have you. You are so tiny; you can jump around with the little people".

They assigned Mother to a school "way out in Bealsville." Sometimes she stayed in Bealsville during the week and came home on the weekend. Sometimes I went with her and sometimes I stayed with grandmother and "the family". The school would have little programs and I gave my speech suitable for a two-year-old. "My name is Doris Ross and I live at 1335 Green Street in Tampa Florida". Then I would bow and walk off the stage.

Mother then accepted a position at Lomax Elementary and Lomax basically functioned as a day care for me. This also meant my education began at about three or four years old, earlier than normal.

In Mother's classroom, I quickly became the class pet. The other children in the classroom were always pulling on me and wanting me to sit with them. One of my most vivid memories is of one special May Day celebration when I was about three years old. This year the celebration had a love theme and they decided to make me a cupid. Mrs. Emma Wilson made a costume for me with pink silk underwear, a wing, and a bow and arrow. At the appropriate time, they started telling me to "run out there and shoot your arrow!" To the designer's extreme disappointment, I had broken one of the wings. Looking back on it, I still think it was alright because when I ran out, I was just a little cupid with a broken wing.

I formally started school after a discussion between Mother and another teacher. Mother said she was going to take me somewhere after school when Mrs. Eva B. Hamilton responded, "Clemmie, why don't you bring her back

Clemmie Ross James teaching at Lomax Elementary

tomorrow and put her in my class?" I was a nice little girl, so she did and before long I was a regular first grade student. When the class got promoted to second grade, I was also.

My mother was always singing and reading stories and poems to me because she was working on making her dream come true. She had a little girl named Doris and she was molding her into a teacher. She constantly looked for ways to broaden my educational experiences; taking me to see Helen Keller was one such event. I was in such awe of what I saw that day; I have since read her biography several times.

Miss Wilson was my 2nd-grade teacher, and I was fascinated with her because she wore a red tam to school every day. Mother had no choice but to buy a little red tam for me. Mrs. Wilson put my tam on my head at the end of each day and made sure it tilted just like hers. I was a motivated second grader and was promoted to third grade along with my older peers.

During the summer, Mother would go to Tallahasse to attend Florida Agricultural and Mechanical College (FAMC now FAMU). Being black she couldn't go to Tampa University, which was around the corner from our house. Since she graduated from Edward Waters College she wanted to go somewhere different. She took me with her, and I benefited from the teaching laboratories. These laboratories positioned me to keep up with students older than myself when I returned to Lomax Elementary.

This was a blessing for mother and me, because a many people couldn't afford to go to college. Having to travel out of the area to attend any college that would admit black students was too expensive for most people.

My mother was my third and fourth-grade teacher and she was very hard on me. Shortly before she died, Mother said to me, "Everybody says I'm such a nice person as a teacher but you Doris!" I replied, "You were rough on me, Mother!" During school, Mother often pinched or pulled on me for something I had done. After school, she would explain, "I have to do that, Doris, so that the other children would not think I was treating you special." She would sometimes buy ice cream or cookies to make up for it.

Later, I became a resource teacher. Once, when presenting at Mother's school, I laughingly told her, "I'm gonna get you back now." She would stare at me and at the end of the day she would say things like, "Doris you did really well, but you stuck your tongue out too much." Or "You said 'ah' too much". I said, "Well Mother, what did you get out of whatever I was saying?" She would say, "You did really well. Now show me how to write those behavior objectives you were talking about." My cousin Susie was in my classes and would say similar things. She would say, "Now show me how to do this again."

When I was ten years old, I was selected to represent the sixth grade in the May Day queen competition. Mother had a girl running for her class, but my class raised the most money and I won. My aunt had a cute short haircut and to my mother's horror, I asked her to cut my hair like hers. She was my mother's younger sister who was only twelve or thirteen years my senior. Well, the queen's crown was too small for my thick and curly hair and Mother was asked to put a warm comb through it to flatten it and make it smaller. It worked and lasted long enough for the coronation. That was the first time I had my hair straightened.

I attended Booker T. Washington Junior High School. Now it would be called a middle school for grades seven to nine. Sometimes the Hillsborough County Health Department personnel would visit our school for special discussions with children about certain developmental stages, which I was not allowed to attend. I never got a chance to hear what they were talking about because I was too young. Mother would tell me everything I needed to know anyway, so I didn't care.

To get to Booker T. Washington, we had to ride a streetcar using tickets the transportation department sold to students. Mother, had an account with Golden Key Grocery Store, one of the stores in that area where we would get off and buy "goodies." I don't remember anything too exciting about attending Booker T except maybe joining the chorus. What did stand out was Mother being protective of me and not wanting me to get off the streetcar at the store for fear of my getting run over. She didn't like the idea of me crossing a very busy street to get to back to school. There was good reason to worry for I had already been run over by Aunt Leola when I was about five years old. She insisted, I eat in the school lunchroom. I, on the other hand, grew fond of a hot sandwich called "carioca," prepared with ground beef in tomato sauce and mustard on Cuban bread. They were exceptionally good, and you could only get them in Ybor City. They don't make them anymore.

Mother almost became the Rosa Parks of Tampa's streetcars. One day the streetcar was crowded, and two white men were sitting in the back, even though there were empty seats in the front. Mother asked the white men to please move up so she and I could sit down. One man got up and the other took his leg and put it across the seat. My tiny mother pushed his leg over, shoved me into the seat, and then sat on the end. A group of domestic workers on the buss who witnessed this scene, clearly disapproved of the man. Fearing them, he got off a couple of stops later.

At thirteen, I went to Middleton Senior High School, from which I graduated at age sixteen. There were several reasons my high school days were not as memorable as one would expect. First, I was at least two years younger than my peers and had nothing in common with them. In fact, due to my age, my aunt Ethel took me to the prom. I was only sixteen years old. A sixteen-year-old then was not like a sixteen-year-old today. Today, they look like adults.

The other reason was because Middleton students were moved around quite a bit. The Middleton building which was located near Lomax burned before I was scheduled to attend. Therefore, we attended Booker T. Washington in the morning as a high school. Booker T. Washington functioned as a double session school with junior high students attending evening classes. At one point, we attended school in the old McFarland buildings, located at the corners of Willow, LaSalle, and Laurel Streets, and called it Middleton High School. McFarland was in West Tampa, near my home. During this time, the boys called me "pony express" because I would cut through a field and run home as fast as I could. I didn't have a boyfriend in high school.

    The school district built a new elementary school for white students, and we black students used their old school, which was not efficient at all. For student body programs, we had to use a very small First Baptist Church building which was across the street from the school. Therefore, we didn't assemble as a student body very often.

    There you have it; this was my early educational experience.

May Day at Lomax - Doris Ross is the queen, Julius Rose is the king

Bethune-Cookman College

One joyful day in July 2013, I delivered a speech at the B-BC Annual Alumni Conference where I shared the platform with CNN television network analyst and lecturer, Roland Martin. I talked about my days at Bethune-Cookman College. My speech follows.

"This is a wonderful way to spend the noontime. I greet you with the words 'waahto wahzura', a phrase from one of the languages spoken in Africa and it means beautiful people and that's exactly what you are.

I am elated to be here today sharing with you. It gives me another opportunity to thank God for allowing me to occupy space on this great beautiful wide world.

I was told to speak with you about my experiences at our dear alma mater which included Dr. Bethune, that great woman who brought a dream to reality through her faith in God and desire to help her people. In doing so, I must share a small segment of my early life.

During the early years of 1908 or 9, my mother who was in 2nd grade dreamed of her future daughter named Doris who would be a teacher. She was dreaming of me.

In 1924, my mother's family moved to Tampa, Florida, where she met and married James Ross, a handsome Pullman Porter, who owned a barber shop. A few years later, on March 13, 1927, I was born to the happy couple. That was my second blessing.

My third blessing came by way of the path I traveled to become the teacher my mother had dreamed of.

At a very early age, I began school and graduated from the public schools of Hillsborough County in 1942.

Long before my high school graduation I had decided that I would attend Bethune-Cookman College.

Oak Hill Elementary School where B-CC graduates practiced teaching

Ms. Hilda Turner drove my cousin Rhudine Bowden, Susie Maddox and me to Daytona to enroll in B-CC. Ms. Turner was Rhudine's aunt and a local teacher who was the plaintiff in the class action suit against the school system fighting for equal salaries for teachers. When we reached Bethune-Cookman College, I was in awe! The campus was simply beautiful.

At that time, many of my family members were graduates of FAMC but I was not going there!! I had two good reasons for that decision.

The first reason led back to the mid-1930s when I accompanied my mother to FAMC during the summers as she continued her college studies on campus. She enrolled me, as a student, in the Lucy Morton Training School which was the elementary laboratory school for college students studying to become teachers. It seems like it rained every day in Tallahassee. There were very few sidewalks and the walking paths were wet and slippery. I slipped and fell every day coming from school and my clothes were always full of red clay.

The second reason for attending Bethune-Cookman College was because of the stories Mother Hattie and my aunts told me about their experiences. My grandfather, Rev C.C. Simmons, was an A.M.E. Church minister who pastored a church for several years in Daytona. Three of the children were enrolled in Mrs. Bethune's Boarding School, Daytona Industrial School for Girls. My grandfather and grandmother were friends of Mrs. Bethune and supported her school. They were also involved with her in civil rights efforts. When Mother Hattie was hospitalized, Mrs. Bethune walked beside the gurney as she was wheeled in to have surgery, singing "Leaning on the Everlasting Arms" (B-CC's shibboleth and the school's watch word).

At B-CC, I found myself under the wings of an anointed woman, Mary McLeod Bethune. I intended to complete the two-year program but, as fate would have it, B-CC became a four-year college. I was present as an alumnus when it was announced that the accreditation requirements had been met to become a four-year college with approximately five areas of study.

I was able to continue at B-CC and obtained a Bachelor of Science Degree. That degree was signed by Dr. Bethune in June 1947 and has a very special place in my home.

Today, my daughter Clemmie rejoices when she points out my diploma and says "See, it's actually signed by Dr. Bethune." Then I chime in and say, "Yes, it came directly from her beautiful hand to mine." Yes, I have seen B-CC rise from a two-year junior college to the University it is today.

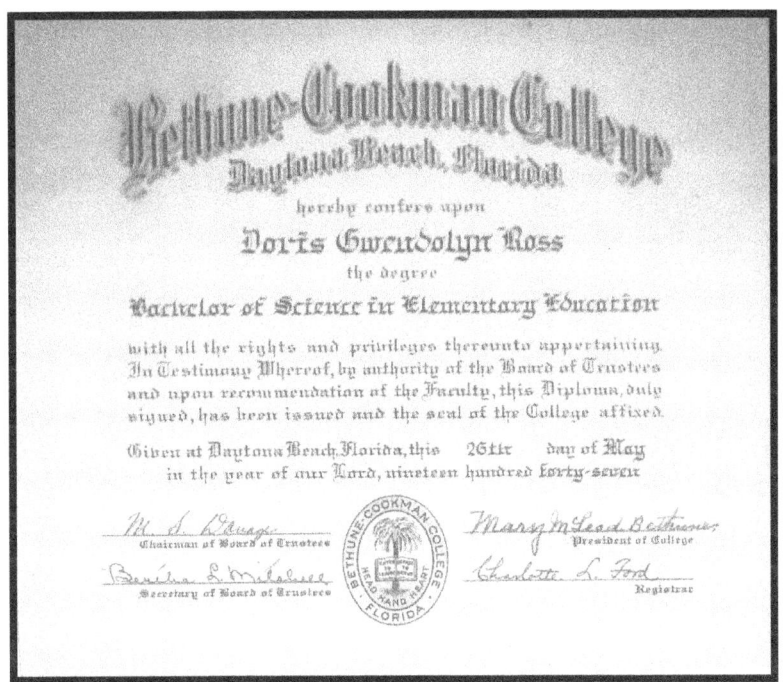

Doris Gwendolyn Ross Bachelor of Science in Elementary Education - Diploma signed by Mary McLeod Bethune

At B-CC, students felt a personal touch. There was a caring spirit, and hands-on approach to ensure that students would be successful.

As an example, at the close of the first day's class, Charlotte Ford, my Introduction to Education instructor, gave us the assignment to read the four Gospels in the King James Version of the Bible Matthew, Mark, Luke, and John. We were then asked to write a short narrative stating the characteristics of Jesus as a teacher. During the next session, Ms. Ford called attention to the shy little girl in the corner saying, "The timid little girl wrote an excellent paper." I was that shy girl. Ms. Ford became my mentor and worked with me throughout my stay at B-CC.

Highlights:
The new student orientation included the traditional "Funeral Service for Gossip", held in the quadrangle, located near White Hall. Gossip was buried and was not to rise from the grave. As we buried gossip, we heard how it could kill, how it could get you in trouble, and all the other evil things gossip could do. It had to be eliminated.

The guiding principles students are learning today; I also carry in my heart. I "entered to learn and departed to serve." And served is what I did. I used my head, my heart, and my hands to help my people in any way I could.

We wore uniforms on and off campus. We wore them to church and the movies. We went in groups and with chaperones.

Community Meetings: Every Sunday, the entire staff, and student body came together to perform for the community including wealthy Caucasians from Ormond Beach. There was an organized processional with line captains accounting for everyone via a roll call. We marched into White Hall single file, wearing our blue and white uniforms and stepping to Mrs. Hacker's and Miss Graham's music. Because it was during World War II and the young men were soldiers, and at war, we sat in every other seat to give the appearance of being a larger group. White Hall was our administrative building and auditorium, used for socials, graduations, and presentations by famous people. We heard dignitaries like Marjorie Stewart Joyner, Zora Neale Hurston, Langston Hughes, George Washington Carver, First Lady Eleanor Roosevelt, and many others. Faith Hall was our dining hall. Curtis Hall was a three-story girl's dormitory. Cookman Hall, initially a boy's dormitory, was divided into boys and girls to accommodate the increased girls' enrollment. The Harrison Rhodes building was our Library.

One Faithful Day: A few days after enrollment at B-CC, some friends and I were sitting on the big white benches on the lawn near White Hall when we saw a stately lady approaching us with her head held high, swinging her cane, and with an obvious air of importance. She said, "Good morning my lovely young ladies." We said, "Good Morning." She repeated her greeting with increased firmness in her tone. "Good morning girls." We repeated our response. Then with undeniable power behind her words, she said: "GOOD MORNING GIRLS!!! She firmly believed important people deserved respect. This lady was Mrs. Mary McLeod Bethune, and we sprang to our feet and gave her the respect she was due.

Family Connection: My grandmother (Mother Hattie) and Mrs. Bethune were born during the era when both families desired an education. Great Grandmother Jane Sherman did not get one, but her children did. As a slave, she often said she could play with the white plantation children but was told never to touch books. As a free adult and parent, she said her children had to go to school so they could see what was in those books the white people didn't want them to see. Hearing her mother's words, Mother Hattie and Rev. Simmons enrolled three of their children in Mrs. Bethune's Daytona Industrial School for Girls.

As I conclude my visit with you, I offer this poem to you:

"A Bag of Tools"

Isn't it strange?
That princes and kings,
And clowns that caper
In sawdust rings,
And common people
Like you and me
Are builders for eternity!

Each is given a bag of tools,
A shapeless mass,
A book of rules;
And each must make-
Ere life is flown-
A Stumbling block
Or stepping stone.

RL Sharpe

Dr. Bethune was a person who made steppingstones, and you have gone from her stepping stones to your own. What is my proof? You are here today. I am here because you are me and I am you, and Dr. Bethune lives on in all of us. Being with you this afternoon again gives me another opportunity to thank God for allowing me to occupy space in his great big wonderful world!! May God bless each of you!

Other B-CC Moments: During l my junior or senior year, I joined the Cavalier Cavelettes Club, and they entered me in the Miss Bethune-Cookman contest, which I won.

A lasting and tragic connection to history was Harry T. and Harriett Moore's daughter, Annie Mae Moore, who was one of my "attendants" as a part of my Miss B-CC coronation court. In 1951, about five years after graduation her home in Mims Florida was bombed and her parents were killed. Her father, Harry T. Moore, was a NAACP Civil Rights field organizer who registered massive numbers of blacks to vote. Evangeline, her sister, was on the train in route home and only learned of the tragic event upon arrival. Annie Mae was at home and survived because she was sleeping in Evangeline's bed, away from the window.

B-CC President Dr. Trudi Kibbie Reed honoring Doris Ross Reddick at her 60th Class Reunion in 2006

A Family of My Own

Doris Ross Reddick

Mr. Charles Perry

In 1946, I met this handsome young man, the father of my three beautiful children. He was a recent Tuskegee Institute Physical Education and History graduate who had just arrived in Florida. Mr. Charles Perry moved to Plant City, Florida from Detroit, Michigan where he had been recruited by the Detroit Gems, becoming one of the first blacks to play professional basketball. He traveled with the team during complete segregation, meaning there were no places where he was permitted to sleep or eat along with his teammates. He often had food brought to him on the bus by his white teammates. He ate and slept on the bus. Sometimes, he was told to go "round to the back to the tearoom (like a kitchen)." It was awful for him. Often, the team managers had to search for hosts in the black neighborhood.

On the court, it was a different story. He excelled in multiple sports, including tennis (uncommon for blacks at that time), and football as well as basketball. He broke his knee in Chicago on Soldier Field, giving him lifetime bragging rights.

Charles heard about jobs in Hillsborough County from one of his Tuskegee Institute contacts. He wanted to settle down, so he and this friend, William Bethel, moved to the Tampa Bay Area. They were later joined by another friend, Fred Fuller. William and Fred settled in Tampa. Charles moved to Plant City, a small town that is a stone's throw from Tampa. He lived with a wonderful family, Edgar and Alice Lewis, who were friends of my mother even though this friendship played no role in our meeting.

The three Tuskegee graduates, and would-be lifetime friends, eventually became successful and renowned coaches in the Tampa Bay area.

I had just finished college and, at that time, people in Plant City were on the "Strawberry School" schedule. These students were out of school in the winter, instead of summer, so they could work the fields in the winter picking strawberries. During the summer, teachers were away taking courses themselves, in schools like Bethune-Cookman College, which led to a shortage of summer school teachers in Plant City.

Since teachers were needed for the students/workers who attended school in the summer, Mother received a call offering her an opportunity to work. She declined the offer but said her daughter had just finished college and would be delighted to hear about it. I was and accepted my first job as a Strawberry School teacher, I and reported to work at Simmons Elementary.

I was not placed at the same school as Mr. Perry; he was at the high school. I was assigned to a school held in two little houses, for first through third-grade students. I taught second-grade students.

On one faithful day, I had to go to the "big school" (now known as Marshall High School) for a faculty meeting. Mr. Smith was the principal of both schools as he was responsible for first through twelfth grades. That day a tall, handsome, well-built gentleman came in and sat right behind me. He passed a note to another friend asking if I was his girlfriend. His friend said no and that was all Mr. Perry needed to hear.

Doris Ross Perry & Charles Perry

He said a word or two to me, but I don't remember what they were because I was only interested in what the principal was saying. I concentrated on my new job, and new experience for me and I was totally focused on the task at hand.

One day as I sat on the bus waiting to depart, he tapped on my bus window and said he wanted to take me and my friend, Alma Smith, to Tampa. This was a strange offer since he didn't have a car at the time. The next day there he was again. We started talking and became good friends. The relationship mushroomed from there.

His seriousness became apparent when he told me that he wanted a car and wanted to pay cash for it. He asked me to hold the money until he could I save enough to buy it. People don't give their money to just anyone. He purchased his car as planned. It was a dark blue Mercury, and he was so proud of it. Now he could drive to see me on Green Street anytime.

We married early one morning in 1948. Neither of us wanted a big wedding. We got a marriage license and had it for about a month when Aunt Pattie gave me a bridal shower at her hotel, The Robert City Hotel. That night, he came over and said, "Let's get married in the morning." This was entirely possible since my uncle was a minister.

The next day, Mr. Perry arrived all dressed up in his finest. I wore a pretty pea green short dress with matching shoes. Aunt Eva, my cousin Herbert, Aunt Ethel, Johnnie Ward McLeod, my mother, and grandmother were there. My cousin Florine was my bride's maid. Reverend Jones, Aunt Ethel's husband, married us.

Grace Street

My Aunt Eva announced one day, "I know exactly the house for you. It is a house that is newly built." Then she, Mother and my grandmother took me to see the house on Grace Street. They marveled at the white lawn chairs on the lawn and the pretty little Jacaranda tree, in full bloom. I told Charles about it and offered to show it to him. He said he didn't need to see it and that if I liked it, he liked it. All he needed to know was where the papers for him to sign were.

After twenty-five years and raising three beautiful and loving children, I had to make some difficult decisions about the marriage. I still live in the little house on Grace Street.

Doris Ross Reddick on Grace Street

Education Began at Home

Kenneth Perry - My First Born

In 1949, my very good friend Johnnie Ward McLeod and her husband, Rudolph McLeod, had a baby. When I went to the hospital to see Johnnie and her new baby, I took one look at her baby and said, "OOOHHH, I want one of these." Almost nine months to the day from when Cheryl McLeod was born, Kenneth Christopher Perry arrived. In the first picture of Kenneth and me, I looked as if I didn't know what to do with this five-pound human being. I didn't.

At that time, pregnant teachers had to stop working by their fourth month and not return until four months after childbirth. That didn't bother me because I didn't want to leave my baby anyway. We came "home" to Mother Hattie at 1335 Green Street.

As Kenneth grew into a little boy, he and his great grandmother did well together. Mother Hattie taught her great grandson many things. When he started school, we all became his teachers. He attended Helping Hand Day Nursery and Kindergarten.

Kenneth was very smart and always wanted a job. As soon as he was big enough go to the store around the corner, he relentlessly badgered the Montileon family who owned a large market right behind our house, to give him a job. They finally gave in and gave Kenneth a little job weighing fruits and vegetables and delivering groceries in the neighborhood. The owners told me that he did a better job than some of the adult men. Some of the Montileon family became dentists in South Tampa and have worked on my teeth.

At Carver Elementary School, Kenneth became a crossing patrol guard and was assigned to a very dangerous spot. I was extremely disturbed, and when I protested to Mrs. Ruby Smith, I was told they did not have another boy who could do what Kenneth could do. He took his responsibility seriously and did an excellent job. Because of Kenneth's diligence, he was chosen to take to Washington DC for the annual summer trip for school patrol boys.

During the summer, Kenneth taught swimming and was even promoted to supervisor over some adults who had taught him. Some of them tried unsuccessfully to trick him into leaving early one day. His response was, "Oh no, I'm not going to lose my job."

Kenneth went to college and earned a Bachelor of Science in Physical Education. Charles had used his contacts to secure a football scholarship to Tennessee State for Kenneth. However, upon enrolling and attending a week of practice, Kenneth didn't like being at Tennessee State. To his father's dismay, I advised Kenneth to get his clothes and car and drive to FAMU since enrollment would begin the next week. Kenneth did just that and is a proud "Rattler" today.

After graduating from FAMU Kenneth came home and married Jessie Mae McBride, the girl he had been dating since high school. He had my blessings because I had taught her as a child and remembered her as smart and well-mannered. She is a very nice person who is always willing to do anything for me. I couldn't ask for a better daughter-in-law.

Kenneth, with his PE degree, wanted to get his masters and advance to recreation administration, but it just wasn't to be. Every time a desirable position opened, someone else would receive the job or be promoted over him. Then a friend, working in Mayor Sandy Freeman's office, encouraged him to try working for the city. He passed their entrance screening and ultimately completed a 27-year career with the City of Tampa.

His City of Tampa career included being an Equal Employment Opportunity (EEO)/labor relations manager, and a community affairs manager. He also directed collective bargaining negotiations with the Amalgamated Transit Union and non-union organizations and was an acting CEO and chairman of the Board of Directors for the Tampa Bay Federal Credit Union.

After Kenneth's retirement from the City of Tampa, he still wanted to work; he was not happy as a retired person. He returned to the School District to a special program that was ideal for him and the children. Kenneth joined the ATOSS program. Ironically, I played a major role in the development of this program, "Alternative To Out of School Suspension" (ATOSS) is Hillsborough County's suspension amnesty program for students suspended from school as a consequence of inappropriate behavior. ATOSS is a voluntary program and an option that provides behavioral and academic help for one to ten days. Students who successfully complete the program are counted as having full attendance during their time in ATOSS, and they can make up any work they missed upon returning to school.

Post retirement, Kenneth served on a credit union's board and taught children with special needs. True to his nature, he functions as the guardian of our family. He continues to speak for people who are not able to speak for themselves.

Ross Perry – My Creative One

I was an only child and didn't like that so much. I wanted siblings for Kenneth and Kenneth was always asking for a brother to play with. Therefore, seven years after Kenneth was born, my husband Charles and I decided it was time to have another child.

The good news is Kenneth's wish to have a baby brother came true. Unfortunately, he came a little earlier than nature planned. His premature brother, Ross Anthony Perry, could not throw a ball so Kenneth was ready for this baby to go back to where he came from. Kenneth did not realize his new brother had to grow into someone who could play ball with him.

Ross' lungs were not fully developed. At about two weeks old, this condition illustrated his strong will to live. We noticed that every time we put him to sleep on his stomach he would flip over like a fish. We eventually learned from the doctor that his little lungs were being crushed and he could not breathe. His flipping over saved his life. He also never cried because his vocal cords were not developed.

Mother Hattie and Mother were extremely worried. I wasn't because I didn't know enough to be afraid. Mother, who was very aware of retardation, would slap her hands and watch his actions. She would move her head from side to side to see what he would do. Soon enough, Ross would reveal that he was not mentally challenged.

Once Ross started talking, he spoke in complete sentences. One day, Ross was walking through the house and spilling a little too much water for his great grandmother to ignore. In a high-pitched voice, she said, "Ross you are spilling water everywhere!" Ross responded, "Mother Hattie you just get too excited." Via testing, we discovered that Ross had the highest IQ of my children.

By second grade, he was putting his delightful personality to good use. His New York teacher said he did so much to help the class have happy days.

As we watched him constantly tinkering with everything he could get his hands on, Ross' intellect became undeniable. When he was seven or eight years old, he made an intercommunication system in the house. He used old wires, radio parts, and a couple of things I purchased for him. The intercom system went from the back room to the front room of the house. On another occasion, he made a box with bells and took it to his school, George Washington Carver Elementary. You could hear the bells all over the school.

Ross was also interested in space exploration. One day he said to Mother Hattie, "I'm going to go into outer space." She inquired, "Would you give Mother Hattie some of your money?" Ross quickly replied, "No that money would have to go to my wife. If I give you money, I will have to go into outer space three more times." He knew if he gave money to his great grandmother, he would also have to give money to his wife, to me, and his grandmother.

Ross always had a strong desire to learn. I remember he was crying his eyes out and when I asked him why he said, "You won't teach me how to read." That broke my heart, and I took immediate action. Mother gave me some books and I put signs on everything around the house. I labeled chairs, doors, tables and anything else I could. Eventually, it became apparent Ross had a photographic memory. I would open a book to a page he had not seen, let him look at it for a while and ask, "Ready?" When replied yes, I closed the book and he could repeat what he read, word for word.

Ross did very well at Gorrie Elementary and made some lifetime friends. He gave his white friends a non-stereotypical view of black people and he learned the same from them. Along the way he also worked with migrant workers, giving him a balanced cultural exposure.

His life took on new meaning when he went to Germany to support a friend's sports team. There he met Sandra; they married and brought into the world two wonderful children who are the joys of my life. The marriage was not what he hoped it would be, but he takes fatherhood seriously and you can't find a better father than Ross.

Ross always liked listening to music because he heard music at home all the time. I had a piano at one time, even though I didn't play for anyone but myself. He followed his father around and hung out with his father's friends. Charles Perry loved music and frequently listened to the radio or played his record player. He had a wonderful collection which my children still have.

In high school, Ross had a friend who played in a musical group, and he learned they had lost their bass player. Ross agreed to replace him. He had never had a bass lesson in his life or even owned a guitar. He came home and announced to me he wanted a bass guitar. When I asked him why having the instrument was so important, he said he just wanted one. At that time, I didn't have a lot of money to spend on things we didn't need so, I said, "I'll think about it." After that, every other day he would ask me for the guitar. One day he came to me and asked so pathetically, "Ma, are you going to get it?" I said, "Not today, I have a headache." I heard him telephone one of his friends and say, "My mom is sick, and we can't go today, she has a headache." Ross had probably told him he would have a guitar by that day. He was attending Plant High School with affluent children who could get a guitar at a moment's notice. I said to myself, "Oh Lord let me get up and go get this guitar." So, I bought it.

He went to practice with the young people, and they gave him a lesson or two. He became out a wonderful player. Buying the guitar was just the beginning. We were having the carpet replaced when I overheard one of the workers call his boss and say, "He has a whole band of stuff back here. We can't move all of this stuff!" By then Ross had a trumpet and a huge drum set including a massive amplifier. They moved it somehow.

The first time I heard him play was at a little center

in Ybor City called The New Place. They had just gotten started and had a concert. I went. At one point during the performance, I bent down to get something when someone started singing. I looked up, and it was Ross! I didn't even know he could sing at all. It was a great experience to see my son sing and play so well.

In Tallahassee, he joined a group that played in night clubs. Ross would get gigs for the band and was so good at it; he became a star. He was full of rhythm and when they played people shouted, "Get it, Ross. Go, Ross! Ross, Ross, Ross!" The band leader got so upset with everyone was calling Ross' name, he kicked Ross out of the band.

Today, Ross is the owner of Trail Blazers, a computer company.

Clemmie Perry - My Gift

Before I could get back to work after Ross was born, Clemmie was on the way. Ross and Clemmie are only 14 months apart. They were like twins. Mother said, "Oh Doris, your children are so cute, but they are so close. I feel sorry for you because all you do is change diapers and wash bottles."

One of the first things I heard when my baby girl was born was, "This baby looks just like Ms. Clemmie." My mother was one in a million, and my last born looked just like her, so it was predestined for my new baby to be named Clemmie Charlyn Perry. Love for three people was expressed in her name: Clemmie for my mother, "Char" for her father Charles and "lyn" for Ellen, her paternal grandmother.

Clemmie was my surprise baby. We had not planned for her, but she planned for us. It was as if she said to the Creator, "Send me down there to those Perry's, they need me." She came here wanting to show what she could do as early as possible. She could barely walk when she got away from us at a performance, went on to the stage and was so cute she ended up in the newspaper.

One Person Can Make A Difference

Clemmie Perry

She and Ross were named king and queen of the nursery. My little busybody was traveling with the family by train to New York, and somehow, she got OFF the train before we departed. When she was reunited with us, she said, "I thought I was in New York."

In New York, we were stopped in our tracks at her first PTA meeting. Her teacher opened her mouth and said to us, "Clemmie is not going to get promoted to the second grade." We demanded to know how she knew after one short month in school. I don't remember what she said, but our feeling was "That lady didn't do anything but lie." I told Mother, and she sent me all the first-grade books.

Doris Ross Reddick

Clemmie Perry

Clemmie was a tomboy who played football every day. The moment she arrived home from school, it was normal to hear her say, "Come on Ross let's play." With our new family mission to get Clemmie through the first grade, the football games with the boys were over. Clemmie had to come in and do her homework. I worked with her until I tired and gave her to her dad; he worked until he tired then Kenneth and then Ross took their respective turns. She ended up at the top of her class.

Oddly enough, Clemmie developed into a curriculum development executive for major corporations. Teaching is in her DNA. Can you imagine that?

Clemmie combined the best of her dad and me because she excelled in athletics as well as academics. She was one of the first two professional black cheerleaders for the Tampa Bay Buccaneers and later the Miami Dolphins.

Today, Clemmie is Founder and Chief Executive Officer

of Women of Color Golf (WOCG contributing to the legacy of progressive women in this family. From a set of abandoned golf clubs, she built an organization that earned her an invitation to the White House. There, she witnessed President Barack Obama present a Presidential Medal of Honor to legendary golfer Charlie Sifford. Her golf initiative would have pleased her multi-sport playing, coaching father. The fact that she develops curricula for golf education makes me smile.

Doretha Edgecomb and Clemmie Perry at NCNW's annual banquet following Clemmie's speech. Edgecomb, one of my elementary school students, served on the Hillsborough County School Board following my departure. She is the second African American woman to serve on the board.

Doris Ross Reddick

Ross, Kenneth and Clemmie Perry

L-R: Ross, Harold, Doris, Clemmie, Kenneth, and Clemmie James (seated)

Standing L-R: Ryon, Emily, Clemmie; Seated L-R: Ross, Doris, Kenneth

Doris Ross Reddick

Norene Copeland Miller

Norene Copeland Miller considers me a blessing in her life; however, it has been a blessing for me to be a part of her amazing personal growth over the last thirty years.

Harold and I met Norene at St. Paul United Methodist Church because of its Roa's Ark after school program. Norene's children loved Roa's Ark and church body diversity. The interaction provided a rich experience for them to learn from Hispanics and other cultural groups at the church.

In 1985, I decided she would be one of my chosen daughters. I did my best to encourage her family to join the church, and they did. Not only did Norene join the church, she was also appointed the Director of the Resource Center and as my assistant. She assisted me with the aerobics and GED classes we offered to the community.

I saw in her a struggling young mother with a strong desire for self-improvement. I took her under my wing, encouraged and motivated her to continue her education.

Over the last thirty years, Norene took that encouragement and ran with it. She has earned a Bachelor of Arts Degree, two Masters of Science Degrees is a Certified Mediator, and Florida Supreme Court 13th Judicial System and

Registered Mental Health Counselor. Norene says I made a positive impact on her life that will last forever. I say Norene's perseverance makes me feel that indeed one person can make a difference in another person's life.

To my children, the words I wrote to you on December 23, 2001, are still true and heartfelt. I offer them to you again today:

"To Kenneth, Ross and Clemmie Perry... and Norene"
My Dear Children,
Just think, you're here not just by chance but by God's choosing. His hands formed you and made each of you into the persons you are.

Clemmie, Ross, Kenneth, and Norene remember that He compares each of you to no one else. You know it is a fact; therefore, consider yourself not just special but exceedingly special because you are each one of a kind.

My dear children keep the faith and trust Him. You don't lack anything that God's grace cannot give you. He has allowed you to be here on this earth, in this family at this time in history to assist in the fulfillment of His special purpose for this generation.

Each of you has an obligation to God, to yourselves, to each other and to humanity to do your part in the accomplishment of His will.

I pray that you will follow the inner spirit God has placed within you. By doing so, you will enjoy much peace, love and happiness. I love you much and much more!

My Grandbabies

Doris Ross Reddick, Emily & Ryon Perry

Ryon Charles Perry is my first-born grandson and my "heartbeat". I was in my late 70's when he was born and because he is such a delightful child, I call him my "heartbeat". Ryon carries his grandfather Charles Perry's name and he has heard a great deal about him from his father, Ross. He is academically smart, athletic and wise beyon his years. Like his father and grandfather, he has excelled at football and basketball. He is an excellent writer, and we hope he will continue telling the family stories. He revealed his literary interest and talent when reviewing an early version of this memoir. Though only nine-year-old, Ryon read it as if he was an adult.

Four years earlier he had written this:

"Dear Grandma:
You are the best grandma I could ever have.
I can name so many reasons how nice you are. Here are some:

Reason#1 you help me with stuff.
Reason #2 you help when Clemmie tries to do sneaky stuff. You say "Clemmie don't do anything to my grandchild."
Reason #3 you do all kinds of cool recipes with me.
Reason #4 you give me good ideas for things we can do together.
Reason #5 you do a lot of playing with me and it is super fun.
Reason #6 you give me good idea."
Ryon

Emily Danielle Perry is my beautiful and talented granddaughter. She has inherited the family "teacher gene" and loves to hold "classes" for the adults in the household.

She became fascinated with her cousin Naima's drawing which hung in my home office and it inspired her to draw. In fact, by eight years old she was producing fashion designs like a professional.

Emily was at the dentist's office with me when she asked me to open my mouth. She drew my opened mouth with all my teeth illustrated. She is a great artist.

Her favorite story is the one about how her dad, Ross, got into our car as a little boy and how her granddad had to run outside in his underwear to stop the car from hitting something across the street.

Doris Ross Reddick

Ross Perry, Doris Ross Reddick, Ryon & Emily Perry

With Ryon and Emily's mother, Sandra, being German, they have dual citizenship and often travel to Germany. These experiences with their mother, along with the Perry, Ross and Reddick family legacies, offer my grand-babies a brightly lit path to the future.

My marriage to Mr. Harold Reddick (more about him later) came with some truly precious gifts. His son, Harold Reddick II and his wife Phyllis gave me two additional lovely granddaughters, Jamaica and Naima Reddick. Beautiful, talented and super smart defines them both. Naima is attending Cornell University in New York on a Fine Arts Scholarship, and Jamaica is a drama major attending Rollins College in Winter Park, Florida.

Norene Miller, my chosen daughter and friend, shares her four children with me to love as grandchildren. Norene is making history in her own right, and I am very proud of her.

I love all my grandchildren dearly.

One Person Can Make A Difference

Naima Reddick

Jamaica Reddick

Mother/Daughter Love

MOTHER DEAR – Clemmie Ross James

Harold Reddick told me that he wished he knew what made me tick. Getting to know my mother unlocked that mystery for him. Mother is so much a part of my story; I must tell a part of her story. Since I was an only child, Mother was my mother, my father, my sister, my brother and my friend. If you knew her, you know me.

Following is the speech I delivered during my visit to Clemmie Ross James K-8 School for their first staff meeting of the 2004-2005 school year:

> "What a wonderful way to begin my day! Thank you for inviting me to this historic occasion. I am extremely excited about the new concept that our school district selected the Clemmie Ross James K-8 Grades School to proceed with.
>
> Mr. Jeff Millman, my family and I are very grateful for the beautiful t-shirts and for the information you have shared with us about the intent of the educational program that will be in place at this school. Involving the faculty, staff, students, parents, business and community members will certainly be the ingredients necessary for a strong school family. We, Mrs. James' family, consider it an honor to be a part of this school's family.
>
> Harry and Rosemary Wong, in their work on effective teaching, say there is only one first day of school. It signals a new beginning: a new principal, a new program structure, new co-workers, new students, etc., to accomplish your vision and mission as you encourage students to be the best that they can be.
>
> As things of the past are left behind, I am reminded of a little rhyme Mrs. James often recited to her students,
> 'You cannot change yesterday.
> That is clear
> Nor begin on tomorrow
> Until it is here
> So all that is left
> For you and for me,
> Is to make this day
> The best it can be!'
>
> Again, I say to you, Mr. Milman and staff, please know that your kindness in sharing your very first day with my son

Kenneth and me, the organization of the Clemmie Ross James K-8 School, named in memory and honor of my mother, a people's person who dearly loved teaching children.

My entire family and my friends wish all of you a very successful start to a new school year. We know you can and will be very effective because each of you is destined for accomplishment, engineered for success, and endowed with seeds of greatness."

On Saturday August 10, 1997, this presentation, Her DASH, was part of the Commencement Celebration for Mrs. Clemmie Ross James at Allen Temple A.M.E. Church, for she had graduated from her earthly duties. The speaker was Alva Simmons.

HER DASH:

Reverend Graham and associates, members of this great church, friends, my friend Doris and this loving family, I consider it an honor and a privilege to share with you, just a few of the momentous experiences in the life and time of Clemmie Ross James, November 3, 1901-(HER DASH) August 6, 1997:

In Quitman, Georgia just past the turn of the century, on November 3, 1901, a beautiful baby girl was born to an African Methodist Episcopal minister and his wife, The Reverend C.C. and Hattie Sherman Simmons. Interestingly enough, this child was named after another A.M.E. minister, The Reverend Clemmons Tillman, a loyal Christian servant. His character traits were such that this child's parents desired those same admirable and charitable qualities for their precious first born. They named her Clemmie and dedicated her to God.

Clemmie's early years were spent in Lake City, Daytona, Palatka and Jacksonville, Florida. At age 11, she was converted and united with Mt. Moriah A.M.E. Church, which of course it was pastored by her father.

Clemmie attended private and public schools and graduated from the high school division of Edward Waters College. She earned a Bachelor of Science degree from Florida A&M College.

Following the death of her father in 1924, Clemmie along with her mother, sisters and brother, moved to Tampa. Right away, Clemmie became a member of St. Paul A.M.E. Church. Shortly thereafter, this charming, charismatic young lady met another charmer, Mr. James Ross. After a brief courtship, they married in 1925. Clemmie Ross joined her husband in worship at Allen Temple where she remained. The couple's only child, Doris, was christened there.

Over the years, Clemmie served her Lord by giving of her time, talents and resources. She served as a Sunday School Teacher and as a member of the choir, A.C.E. League, and the Missionary Society. With a winning contagious smile, she was also a morale booster for her church's membership and others. Some years after the death of Mr. Ross ---- guess what? Clemmie married another Allen Temple member, Mr. Enoch James. That was in 1936.

This pioneer educator began her teaching career at an elementary school, "a strawberry school" in eastern Hillsborough County community known as Bealsville (Plant City), Florida. After a while, she was assigned to Lomax School in Tampa where she taught for more than 40 years. She was dedicated. In her roles as friend and mother figure, she influenced the lives of hundreds of children and adults. At Lomax Mrs. James also served as assistant principal to Mr. John Clarke.

This dynamic lady was one of Tampa's early advocates for human dignity for all people, especially the under-served. She worked diligently with several civil and equal rights organizations including the National Council of Negro Women, NAACP, Health and Education Association and Retired Teachers Association. She also volunteered as a political worker.

Beginning in the late 30's, Mrs. James was one of the forerunners and strong supporters in of the struggle for equal pay for black teachers in Hillsborough County. This goal was finally achieved in the mid 40's and she received many accolades for her efforts.

Lastly, throughout her long, illustrious and productive life, God used Clemmie Ross James as a missionary of mercy, hope and goodwill. Her outreach of goodness and abundant love are integral parts of Tampa's folklore. Wednesday, August 6, 1997, was commencement time for Clemmie. Her serene, peaceful passing was characteristic of the way she lived her life, with a quiet dignity and unwavering faith in God. Even at the end of her earthly journey, she was teaching a lesson. Doris said, and I quote, "My mother taught me how to live and she most certainly taught me how to die."

1901 "DASH" 1997 Presenter: Altamese Golden Simmons

Completing Mother's biography, these excerpts are from my "Testimonial to Mrs. Clemmie Ross James" presented at a meeting of the National Council of Negro Women (NCNW), on Monday December 19, 1983. The theme of the meeting was "Willingness is an Open Door to Achievement." The following was from Mother's biographical sketch:

> "More than 30 years ago, a group of concerned women, under the leadership of the late Mrs. Fanny Ponder of St. Petersburg, Florida, revitalized the Tampa metropolitan chapter of the National Council of Negro Women. Clemmie James was one of those wonderful women. [To date there are four generations of NCNW members in our family - my grand Aunt Pattie, my mother Clemmie, myself and my daughter Clemmie].
>
> As a young adult, Clemmie's first employment was as a receptionist for Cole's Transfer Company. Soon thereafter she received a teaching position with Hillsborough County Schools at Lomax Elementary School, where she served for 40 years.
>
> Her affiliations are: Allen Temple Missionary Society; NAACP, Health and Education Association; Order of Eastern Star, Fitz Patrick Chapter #6; Lily White Security Benefit Association Royal Court; Grand Union Pallbearers; United Methodist Women's Group; Tampa's Local and Retired Teachers Association; AARP; National Council of Negro Women; Advisor, National Council of Youth Group; and National Council Young Adults."

Now you know why I was so inspired and driven. My tiny mother was enormous in my life.

Following are letters affirm the love we shared, first a letter from me to my mother, Clemmie Ross James. The second letter, from my daughter Clemmie Perry to me, reveals that love moved down another generation.

Clemmie Sherman James
Doris Ross Reddick - Clemmie Perry

Doris to Mother Clemmie

Mother Darling,
    I'm not giving you one of those fancy cards this year because I want you to know the words, I have in my very own heart for you.
    First, my darling, I want you to know that you are the most wonderful woman in the world, and I thank God for you. I want to ask your forgiveness if I've ever done or said anything to make you unhappy or to cause you to feel that I have not grown to be the type of adult you want me to be. With all my power, I've tried to keep you as my pattern and although I cannot be as perfect as you are, I try hard to be as nearly like you as I can.
    Mother, you have no idea how much I love you and how proud of you I am. You are everything .... and I thank God daily that he gave you to me. I know, there are many nice mothers around, but believe me darling, there is not another mother in the world anywhere like you and just think, you are mine.
    Darling, I want to tell you how grateful I am for the wonderful childhood you gave me and for all the many nice things you did for me to make me the happiest little girl in Tampa. Then I want to thank you for the way in which you handled me and my little problems during my teenage years and above all, I want to thank you for all the wonderful examples you yourself have displayed for me.
    Darling, I want to thank you for instilling within me, your wonderful philosophy of Jesus and his powers and his love for all who trust Him. By doing this, you have led me to know "the light of God surrounds me. The love of God unfolds me. The power of God protects me. The presence of God watches over me and wherever I am God is." Because you have caused me to take this as my philosophy, I have been able to withstand all of the problems which have come up in my adult life and knowing I have God and you on my side I feel that I can conquer anything, and the credit goes to you my darling. You're an angel.
    I want you to know that I thank you so much, not only for the uncountable things you've done for me but for your earnest prayers, your loving thoughts, your honesty, your insight, your understanding, your feelings for others, your beautiful self and for all that beauty which lies beneath your skin which radiates and touches everyone who comes in contact with you. I thank God, that you are not just my mother but.... something special to everyone.

With my entire heart darling, I cherish you and again I thank God for the privilege of being your daughter and may I always prove worthy of your love because that would make me the happiest girl in the world.

It's almost impossible, Mother, but please pray that I shall be the mother to my children that you have been to me.

With all my love, Doris

Daughter Clemmie to Doris:
February 20, 1998

Dear Mother,
As you approach your 71st birthday, I find it so hard to believe that 40 years have passed between us. It seems like yesterday that I was still a little girl in your arms, climbing in your lap, or doing something silly. So often, I long for those days and cherish the beautiful memories.
You have been and are a wonderful inspiration to me. I look up to you with adornment and still find it hard to believe all of the outrageous accomplishments you have made in your lifetime. Sometimes it's overwhelming! Even when I speak about you to other people, they can tell that I cherish your every breath! ....
I have your Hillsborough County School Board picture on my desk at work to remind me daily of what kind of background and backbone I am from! I get so many compliments on the photograph. People say, "She looks like an ambassador or some special dignitary." I laugh and say, "Yes she is a dignitary, she is my mother!" ....
Mother, thank you for being such an inspiration in my life and I hope I have been the kind of daughter to you, as you were to Granny. .... You are the Love of my Life and I am proud of YOU! I only pray that I will become half the woman and mother you have been to us and the children of your community.

Love, Clemmie Perry

Civil Rights for All

A Family Seeking Justice

Doing whatever is within our power to help people is in my family's DNA. Therefore, it was second nature for me to engage in civil rights activities during the sixties. For as long as I can remember and beyond, my family members were in the middle of movements. My great-grandparents were freed via the Emancipation Proclamation and were among the group who wanted to have their children educated. My grandparents, Rev. C.C., and Hattie Simmons worked with the renowned Dr. Mary McLeod Bethune to make life better in their era. They passed this activist spirit on to their children including my mother, Clemmie Ross James. I simply want equality for myself and others, as did my ancestors.

It was a family tradition to subscribe to and read various newspapers, most notably being, the Pittsburgh Courier. Even recently when I informed Kenneth I wanted to discontinue a subscription because I was tired of getting all that paper, he passionately said, "No, we can't do that you've got to read and keep up with the news."

To his point, when I was in elementary school my mother started a movement because of an article she read. The article reported that black teachers made less money than white teachers. As she was a teacher with responsibilities, she needed every penny she could make. She carried the article to school and showed it to Eva B. Hamilton. Mrs. Hamilton was a teacher, the principal's right-hand person and the next person in charge. She gave the article to Principal Ed Davis, and the issue mushroomed from there, ending with a meeting that, unfortunately, was not as fruitful as desired. Principal Davis was fired. He was subsequently hired by the Central Life Insurance Company, a black company. This was my first memory of teacher activism by people close to me.

Years later, during my high school years, inequitable

teacher salaries came up again. This time, black teachers worked with other groups who found themselves in the same situation. They decided to take legal action. In fact, Thurgood Marshall was the attorney handling the case here in Tampa. Hilda Turner, a single teacher who was caring for her niece Rhudine Bowden and living the teacher's salary struggle, volunteered to be named as the plaintiff in a class action suit for equal salaries. Since she taught high school social studies and civics, she was a perfect candidate for the case.

I was extremely interested in this case because of my mother's role, Ms. Hilda Turner being my homeroom teacher, Thurgood Marshall, and the countless teachers in my family who were interested.

Four or five friends, including Doris Lang, Americus Pemienta, Maria Hernandez, and I left school without permission for three days to observe the trial.

Given that I was not in school, I told my mother what I had done. She didn't make a big deal about it. In fact, she was happy about it.

However, one of my teachers, Ms. Frankie Berry, did have a major problem with us missing school. She questioned who gave us permission and when I told her what my mother said, she responded, "We will see about that." Ms. Berry gave a test on material she had covered during our absence on which I made a 35. Mother was more excited about my having seen Thurgood Marshall in action than that single grade.

They won the case. Hilda Turner was the same Ms. Turner who drove Susie Maddox, Rhudine Bowden and me to Bethune-Cookman College. She was the same Hilda Turner who successfully helped us navigate our first day in college and that nerve-racking enrollment process.

During my early teaching days, there was a third effort seeking justice for teachers. Large numbers of both black and white teachers went on strike for several weeks. We walked out of the schools and off our jobs. I was right in the middle of it along with many of my family members. The Hillsborough County School Administration called in substitutes and threatened us with, saying in effect, "If you don't come back by [some designated date], you are going to get fired." We had to go back to secure our jobs. Since so many people in my family were educators and involved with the strike, this was a major threat to us. My mother, my aunts, my husband and I could all have been fired. So, we returned to work.

Later during my career, even with better pay, black teachers and schools still didn't get the educational materials we needed. As a school board member, I went on routine school visitations; what I saw was depressing for many reasons. The fact that one of those distressed schools was named after my mother didn't help. As recent as the 1990s, black school conditions were not good at all. The buses were late. The drains in the ground held stagnant rainwater and loads of mosquito lava. The sidewalks were too small, and the bathrooms were always running over. As I saw it, there was nothing about those schools that would make any child want to come to school. A school in this condition certainly should not represent Mrs. Clemmie James.

I virtually kidnapped the superintendent and his assistant so they could immediately see the horrible conditions firsthand. I told them there was something they must see. Once there, I asked them to explain why these conditions were allowed. They appeared to understand how bad things were. However, reporting to the school board, the superintendent said he didn't see what I saw. My question to him was, "What eyes were you looking out of?" Nonetheless, things were taken care of immediately. Sitting on the school board at that time was challenging, to say the least.

My cousin, Olive Florene Jones, was an educator and community activist. She taught business and Spanish and was an entrepreneur. As a part of an organization called "Young Adults for Progressive Action" (YAPA), she helped organize sit-ins. YAPA was founded by James A. Hammond, Florene Jones, myself, and other like-minded people from the community including Harold Reddick.

YAPA decided to hold a sit-in at the drive-in theater in East Tampa. I didn't go. I stayed home with my children. Indeed, those in attendance were hauled off to jail. Clarence Wilson had his little boy with him which "saved" him from being arrested. They wouldn't take him. Clarence took the boy home and went back to the jail and said, "I belong in there with them."

Mother and I were leaving downtown one day when someone asked if we had seen the kids at the counter. We had not, so we turned around and went back downtown.

Just as the boys did in North Carolina, the young people here in Tampa were having a sit-in at Woolworth, and we were not going to miss it. When we arrived, the first people we saw were mother's nephew, Charles Simmons, and my cousin Florene.

Kenneth, who was about four years old, saw an empty seat and sat in it. One white "servant" (waitress) approached us, and made sure we could hear her said:

"They ought to go back where they came from."

I said, "And where is that?"

She said, "Africa."

I said, "How can you say that when you and I have the same grandfather?"

The woman turned red, my mother pulled me away and said, "Get that child and come on", she said.

I didn't know the lady, and she didn't know if what I said was true or not. I felt comfortable saying that to her because two of my great-grandfathers were white. I can only imagine what questions she asked when she returned home.

Rev. A. Leon Lowry, James A. Hammond, Olive Florene Jones, Harold Reddick and countless others were always a part of equality activities in Tampa. This included bringing Rev. Martin Luther King, Jr. to Tampa. They decided to advance the cause by having lunch at various lunch counters around the city. The members of a large group of people were paired off, and the plan was set. James Hammond and I were assigned to sit at the Legette Drug Store lunch counter which was downtown on Franklin Street.

On the appointed day, I carried a change of clothes to work so that I would be at my best for the event. Hammond picked me up from school and headed for Legette. We sat at a u-shaped counter and had the meal. Some white people who were near got up and moved to another table. That didn't bother us a bit, for we had faith in the undercover people who were watching us. However, I was somewhat nervous and dropped my fork. I picked it up and tried to pretend that nothing happened.

These sit-ins were heartfelt and had deep roots. When Kenneth was little, he would see all this food on the counters and wanted me to buy some. He just couldn't understand why I couldn't and wouldn't allow him to eat any. This was a wrong I wanted to help make right.

Since a young child, I questioned Jim Crow practices, and I couldn't stand the foolishness about colored drinking fountains. I would not drink from anything that said it was for colored people because they may have put something in the water to make it "colored."

Then, Grace Street was bombed! Charles was attending a summer program at New York University, and Mother was away taking a class, so I was home alone. After a class I was taking ended, I didn't want to come home to an empty house. Therefore, I picked up my younger cousins, Al and Charles and my son Ken who was at 1335 Green Street with Mother Hattie. I brought them home with me so they could watch television. That made their day.

As I unlocked the door, I thought I heard a crash. The children didn't hear it, so I dismissed it and prepared snacks for the children.

A few days later, I went into my children's playroom for something. I noticed a blue bottle, with newspaper, and a rag in it, lying on the floor. There was also a stain on the floor beneath the bottle. The broken window confirmed my worst fear. It was a Molotov cocktail! It was a failed bomb!

Now, I was afraid. My family was involved in everything from meetings with Attorney Bill Fordham and NAACP to union meetings, and a lot of people knew it. Bomb threats were common during those days. In fact, my family and I were at Fort Hesterly Armory waiting to hear Martin Luther King speak when a bomb threat was announced to a standing room only crowd. There was an intense search of the building during which a lot of people left. My family and I stayed. Again, we were a part of a history-making moment for Tampa. Therefore, when the bomb was discovered in my home, we didn't call the police because that would have been pointless.

As you know, it didn't stop me from seeking justice.

NCNW social event at Veola Pope's home

A Lifetime of Service

My 57 Years as an Educator Begins

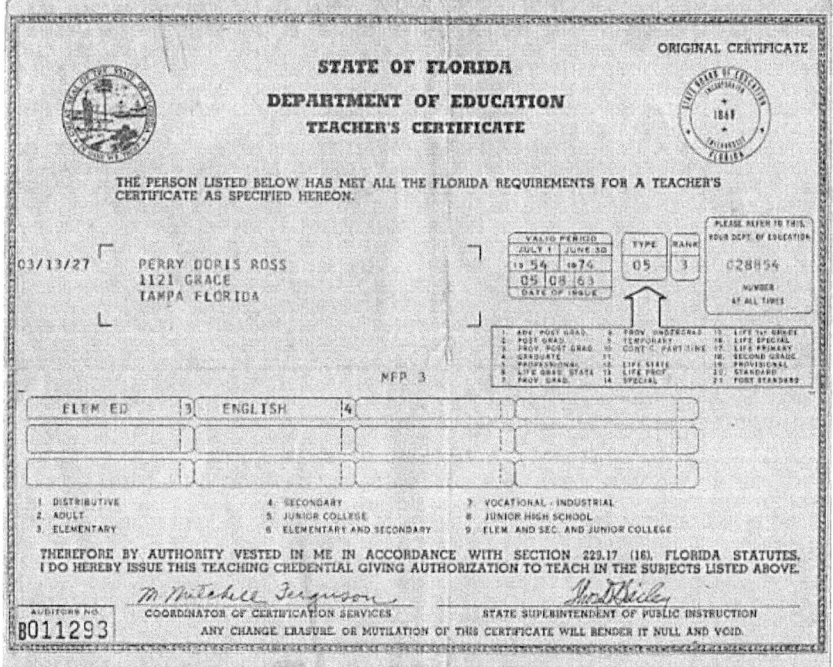

In 1947, the week I graduated from college, I was at home when Mother just happened to get a call from J. Crocket Farnell, a white man, and superintendent of Hillsborough County Schools in charge of all schools. He asked her if she wanted to substitute teach in Plant City. She said, "Well no, I don't but my daughter just finished college, and she may want to do it." So, my first job was as a substitute at Simmons in Plant City, a school in two old duplex-type houses. Simmons was a "strawberry school" because the school accommodated students getting out of school to work in the strawberry fields in the winter and attending school during summer.

My first real assignment was at Dunbar, and I was there for two years. After that, I was sent to Meacham Elementary School, where I taught for a couple of years. Meacham was a six-room elementary school. Principal John W. Lockhart hired me to teach fifth grade.

At Meacham, I learned one very hard lesson. When I heard "Bump, bump, bump" I rudely asked, "Who is that making that noise?" It was a little boy with one leg named Lee. I was so embarrassed. I found it hard to get over that. Because of that incident, I have made it my duty to be fully aware of a situation before commenting.

Soon, when College Hill Elementary School was built for black students, to handle the Lomax Elementary overload, Mr. Lockhart was assigned as principal there. He elected to take some of his most productive people with him and, I was one of them. I helped open the school. I was still a fifth-grade teacher and the chair of the curriculum committee. After this assignment, I went to New York.

In 1963, my husband accepted a job in Kingston, New York, teaching at a boy's school and I accepted a teaching position in Kingston to follow him.

In Kingston, there were several professional and social activities planned throughout the year, including the Kingston Teacher Association's fall dinner, in which new teachers were introduced. Several teachers walked up to me and said, "So you're the new teacher." It was not hard to pick me out of a crowd. There were only three black teachers in the entire district assigned to three different schools. Therefore, they all recognized I was new.

I was assigned to George Washington Elementary School and, I was the first black person some students had ever met. When I walked into the classroom on that first day, it was a historical moment for some of them.

One rather funny thing happened in New York as I was leaving a building one evening. I saw a car approach. It had an antenna on the roof and an insignia on the door. Because I was tired and glad to leave the stress of the day behind, I did not pay close attention to details and waved it down. When the car stopped, I opened the door, got in the back seat, and told the driver to take me to 80 Emory Street. The driver laughed at me and told me, "Well, I can't take you to 80 Emory Street, this is a sheriff's car!" He hailed a real cab driver and told him where to take "this lady." The cab driver said, "You know, I have gotten a lot of patrons from a lot of places, but I have never gotten one from a sheriff's car." I submitted this story to Reader's Digest. They returned it to me unpublished. Well, now I have published it myself!

I was in New York for just over a year before returning to Tampa to take care of some family business. After doing so, I decided to remain in Tampa.

Back To Tampa

In Tampa, I took a teaching position at George Washington Carver Elementary School under Principal Harold Harris. Yes, I went from George Washington Elementary to George Washington Carver Elementary.

I taught a half-day reading class and served as the school curriculum specialist the other half of the day. One afternoon during the curriculum portion of my day, the principal informed me, I had received a call from downtown from Mr. Larry Worden, Supervisor of Elementary Education from "downtown," i.e., ...administrative offices. Mr. Harris suggested they probably wanted to move me from his school and said he would match any offer they made to keep me. They offered me a job as a curriculum specialist and assistant principal at Thonotosassa Elementary School. The Hillsborough County District had five black schools with white curriculum specialists and assistant principals. They wanted to put a black specialist in a predominantly white school since they had none. The schools were slowly being integrated.

At first, I was fearful because I felt this would not be a place for me as a black person after dark. Having to attend PTA and other meetings at night would mean frequent concern for my safety. I started naming other people for them to consider. Mr. Worden told me to go home and think about it. He suggested I go there and that I might like what I found. I followed his advice, and he was right. Over my mother's objections, I accepted the position.

During my introductory period, I went into one of the classrooms, and when the teacher asked the students if they knew who I was, one little girl responded, "Aunt Jemima." I walked over to the child, stooped down to her level and said in my best teacher's voice, "Take a good look at me, okay? If you are talking about the lady on the pancake box, she is a good-looking lady and very smart to come up with pancakes you like. Now go home and if I still look like Aunt Jemima, tell your mother you either need to go to an eye specialist or a psychiatrist. She needs to take you because you are either going blind or crazy." The teacher was visibly alarmed.

I was hired in the late 1960s to teach at Thonotosassa Elementary School and became their first black administrative staff member. As in New York, I was the first black administrative staff member some students, as well as some adults, had ever met.

In this role, I have touched many lives and wonderful children who made me feel blessed to teach.

As a teacher, you can accurately predict the success, failure or even demise of some of the young souls with whom you interact. Some you have no idea how you impact their lives, how they will react to your efforts and God forbid the occasional misbegotten comments directed at them. You agonize over how to shape and reshape their very destiny.

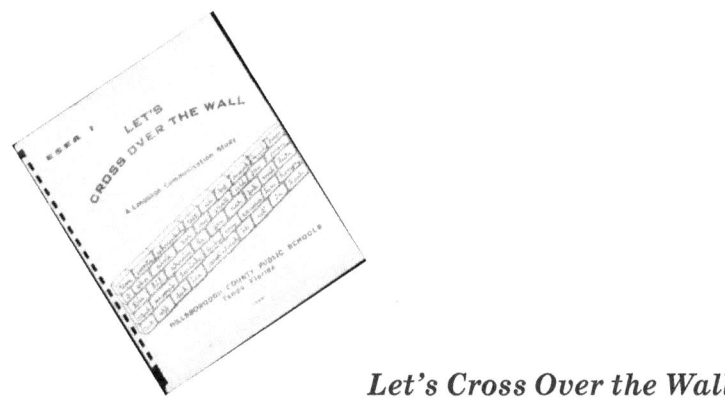

Let's Cross Over the Wall

Integration was not as simple as putting black children in a classroom and opening books. A difficult fact of the time was many black children spoke a dialect that even blacks didn't want to admit existed. In 1969, I co-wrote a book with my friend and fellow teacher, Altamese Simmons; the was named *Let's Cross Over the Wall*.

There was a wall between white teachers and their new black students. We believed some black children spoke a dialect which was really a language unique to American blacks and represented their heritage as descendants of Africans. They were being told that the way they spoke was "wrong." That one word was the root of the problem.

Some teachers felt black dialect was a sign of a mental disability, and I contend they treated black students consistent with their beliefs. I suggest this belief harmed students making them feel they were inferior.

Some students arrived at college never having learned to communicate, because teachers couldn't understand them in grade school and simply ignored them. These teachers could not teach students if they did not understand them and if were not willing to learn. We simply wanted these teachers to go beyond that wall of ignorance by helping them learn a new language that would equip them to teach all students, including those who were black.

A New Beginning

Doris Ross Reddick
Mr. Harold Reddick

Doris Ross Reddick & Harold Reddick

My Prince Charming – Twenty-four years with the love of my life began at a Head Start banquet. I knew who Harold Reddick was but didn't like him. Because I didn't really know him, I thought he was too arrogant. Well, now I know, you can't judge a book by its cover. We officially met at this banquet. He was not in education per se. However, he was associated with nearly everything related to the betterment of people. We were both invited to the event by Mrs. Van Bess. I invited Mother.

Mother, Cecile Essrig and I sat at a table together with one extra seat. Mother looked toward the entrance and said, "There is THE Harold Reddick". I said, "So?" Mother liked him because he WAS into everything. She had seen him many times at various community meetings they had both attended. He walked right over to our table and asked, "Is this seat taken?" Cecile, who knew him very well said, "No, it's not taken. Sit down, Harold." During the evening, he said to me "I'm looking for a secretary, would you be interested?" I said, "Are you kidding; I have a secretary." He said, "I'm sorry." He was such a gentleman that evening; he redeemed himself.

Sometime later, we were having problems with funding for an early childhood program, and we were assigned to talk to people who were the powers-that-be. I was assigned to Harold; I suppose because we were black. I met with him and invited him to the centers. We were concluding a review at George Washington Carver, and since it was lunchtime, Harold asked, "Would you like to go have some juice?" I responded with something about V-8, and he said, "No, I mean fresh juices." I had never had any, so I agreed, and we went to Bertha Laden's. Harold parked his car first. "You can't get in that spot, stop!" he shouted. I said, "You wanna bet!" After that, he would joke about not betting against me on anything.

We married in 1980. At the time, I was the Program Supervisor of the Hillsborough County Early Childhood Program and teaching basic adult education at night in a room provided at Blake High School. I also taught senior citizens in the Bethune High Rise building.

We decided I would stop working because Mr. Reddick was retired and just wanted to do fun things. For the next ten years, we worked on the Roa's Ark program at St. Paul United Methodist Church in Ybor City and traveled with an elder hostel program. I was 52 when I retired and could join Hostel because my husband was retired and a member. We just had a great time.

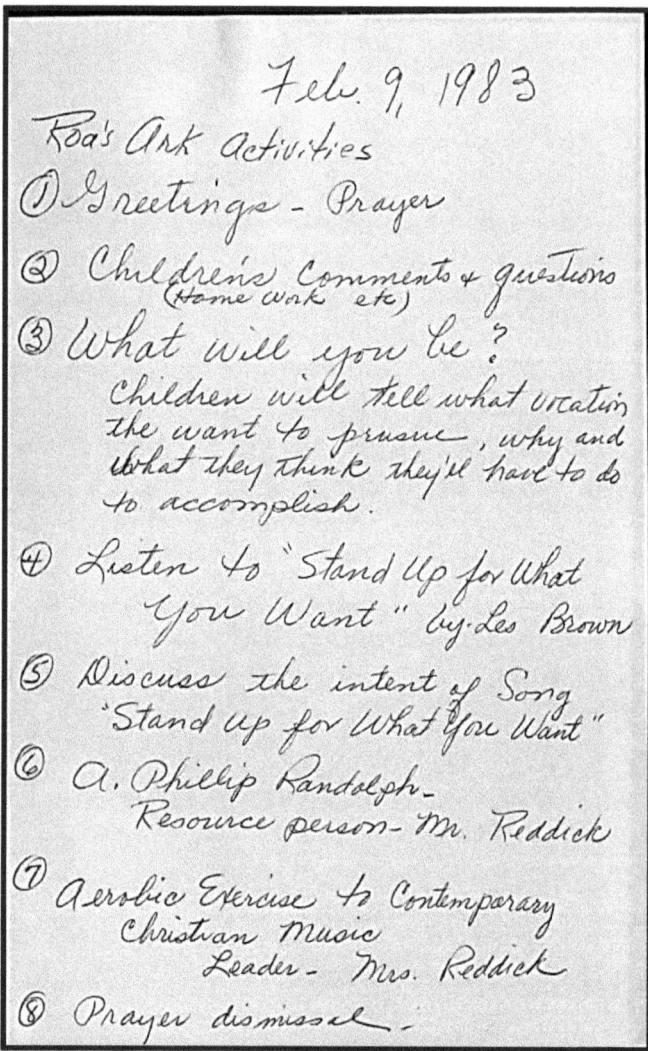

Figure 1 Roa's Ark notes from 1983 (Courtesy USF Reddick Collection)

As for Mr. Harold Reddick, besides being a wonderful person in my life, he has a story that also needs to be told. He was a career "Pullman Porter" and worked as the Area Representative for the Human Resource Development Institute (HRDI AFL-CIO), overseeing job placement in the Tampa Bay Area. He served in the U.S. Army during WWII. He was a VP and negotiator for the Brotherhood of Sleeping Car Porters, a civil rights activist with the Young Adults for Progressive Action, VP of the A. Phillip Randolph Institute, VP of Tampa's NAACP, and an active member of many other key organizations in the Tampa Bay Area.

He was best friends with E. D. Nixon, who bailed Rosa Parks out of jail, and the world-renowned A. Phillip Randolph, founder of the Pullman Porter's Union.

Harold Reddick & A. Philip Randolph

Lawton Chiles

Gov. Jeb Bush and Doris Ross Reddick

Ben Carson and Doris Ross Reddick

Hillsborough County School Board

One Person Can Make A Difference

Standing: Glenn Barrington, Carolyn Bricklemyer, Yvonne McKitrick, Joe Newsome
Sitting: Sam Rampello, Doris Ross Reddick, Carol Kurdell

Campaigning

Campaigning was an interesting experience, and I was well received by the general public. It is a very busy affair, and I learned quite a bit about what it takes to win - hard work!

Together Joe Greco, a friend of mine, and I worked to create a Model City Early Childhood program. He introduced me to Mary Ripper, a campaign consultant in the Tampa Bay Area who knew how to win. John Daniel was my manager. Prudy Manis Calco and my son Kenneth were co-treasurers. It was a wonderfully diverse group of supporters whose help was priceless.

However, during one campaign, a white woman, Rev. Thomas Scott and I were contenders for school board membership. On the day before Election Day, the white candidate placed an ad in news outlets with her picture on one side and Rev. Scott's and my pictures on the reverse side. The caption read, "Which would you prefer?" That statement spoke for itself! I am sure she was surprised when the people preferred me, this pecan-colored woman.

Andrew "Andy" Hurst - 3rd co-campaign manager with Ken

John Daniel
campaign manager

Alva Simmons –
Uncle Jack's granddaughter & a great supporter

Joseph W. J. Robinson - President and CEO of RHCA - Great researcher and campaigner

Joe Greco
Personal and professional friend

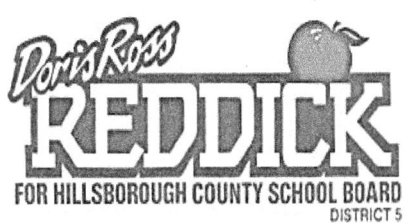

FOR HILLSBOROUGH COUNTY SCHOOL BOARD
DISTRICT 5

Dear Friends of Education,

Education is the keystone of our democratic society. This is a premise that I have supported diligently for many years as a teacher, an administrator, an educational consultant and a school board member. I am writing you today to ask for your continuous support as I seek re-election to the Hillsborough County School Board, District #5.

As you know the population of our county is rapidly expanding. This growth challenges our goals of providing excellence in education for our children. By working together in our community, we can continue this teamwork to protect the future of our children and our schools.

I will continue to work hard to achieve the educational goals that I have championed in the past, but first I need your support. With your assistance we will certainly improve the educational environment for our children and create a stronger democratic system for all citizens.

Please vote for me, DORIS ROSS REDDICK School Board Member District #5

Sincerely,

Doris Ross Reddick

Doris Ross Reddick
Candidate for re-election
Hillsborough County School Board District #5

Decision to Run

Harold and I stayed involved in civic activities. At a fundraiser for Sandy Freeman, Harold was approached about running for Hillsborough County School Board membership. He said, "I am honored, and that would be wonderful for I have always wanted to do something like that, but at this point, my age would be a factor. So, no."
Kenny, a member of the young black organization hosting the event, said to me, "Well if he doesn't, you will have to." I said, "No, I don't. I don't want to do anything like that." I forgot it. A week later, while the family was gathered to have a prayer for Mother, who could barely talk at that point, Kenny came over. He asked, "Are you going to do it, Mother?" I asked, "Do what? Run for office? I don't think so!" I turned to my mother, who had heard the entire conversation and asked, "What do you think, Mother?" As little and frail as she was, she smiled, raised herself up and said in a labored voice, "Go.... for ...it." So, I went for it and won. Mother was able to see me sworn in the first time and campaign for a second term.

Minority Vendor Spending

My lifelong determination to make a difference came from my family's mantra, "Do whatever you can to make the world a better place than you found it." My mission has been accomplished, and it delights me that many are still benefiting from my efforts.

In 1994, shortly after my election as the first black woman to the Hillsborough County School Board, I was presented with a number I was certain was a typographical error. I was told the amount of monies spent with black vendors was just over a thousand dollars. In an entire year, only $1,084 had been awarded to minority businesses. After confirming I had heard correctly, I told the unfortunate person, "It would have been better to report zero than a number as insulting as that."

During my campaign, I was alerted to the inequalities that existed in how allocations were made and that something needed to be done. That became my pet project. At least twice a month at board meetings, I asked for the numbers. All too often I replied "that's not good enough" to the minuscule increases reported.

Inevitably, I began to wear them down because the school board finally hired Derek Myles to address the minority contract allocation disparity issue. However, I was not pleased with his treatment. He was given a very small office, a desk, and chair, a dictionary, two broken down computers and no staff. When I inquired why he couldn't at least be given a working computer, I was told he didn't have computer skills. I was not impressed and not swayed. I argued he should be allowed to attend computer training just as was being done for others.

After Derik Myles' departure, Terrell Jacobs was hired, and he brought very professional new ideas to the table. His goals, however, were not realized because he was "asking for too much." He soon tired of being told "no."

Dr. Edwards then made a sincere attempt to improve the program. Under his watch, the "Pre-Bid Plan" was created and indeed made advances. Each month the numbers would get "a little bit better." Even so, each month I would say, "Thanks, but that's not enough." What ultimately had to be addressed was the lack of awards being given for large jobs with large bonds. Minorities were being excluded because they could not compete with large companies that could easily qualify. The reason cited for this exclusion was the alleged lack of physical offices. They just "couldn't be found." Well, I found two, Harry Howard and Cheikh Sylla. These black architects designed two fantastic high schools, Middleton and Blake schools. Of Mr. Henry Ballard, the long-standing director of the Office of Supplier Diversity, who was in place when I retired, I indeed asked for him because he grew up in a construction business family. He had worked with his father from the time he was a preteen. His father, Henry Ballard Sr., had constructed buildings all over Tampa. There was no doubt Henry Jr. knew the business and had the required degrees. I am very proud of how he embraced this challenge, assembled a staff and acquired the resources to do the job. He diligently and successfully worked at raising minority funding levels. How much? Hillsborough County Schools had spent more than $25 million with minority businesses in 2009 alone.

Minority Vendor Spending
1 person can make a difference

Took some work to turn those Pennies into millions of dollars.

she raised minoirity vendor spending from only $1,084 to $200 million
(averaging $12.5 million per year)

Middleton school Funding

Blake school Funding

Minority Vendor Allocations

Demanding more!

Doris Ross Reddick & Henry Ballard Jr. at his retirement party

As for the total impact of my passion for change, by 2011, the county had spent more than $200 million dollars with minority vendors since the $1,084 of 1994. I feel confident I left the minority business inclusion initiative much better than I found it.

My one regret is Mr. Ballard's compensation was out of sync with his peers in Hillsborough and the surrounding counties. I suggested a public record comparison of diversity directors would have clearly proven my point. Even as you read this, I believe disparity still exists and there is more work to be done.

As grace would have it, something happened just prior to this book going to print that gives me hope for a better tomorrow:

Transcription of presentation of roses to Doris Ross Reddick by Susan Valdez at the Hillsborough County School Board meeting on June 9, 2015:

Susan Valdez: I would like to take this opportunity to recognize the Honorable Doris Ross Reddick, a previous board member from District Five, and she is here today. [Standing ovation]

A few years ago, at a birthday party for Mrs. Reddick, she said a few words that handed a baton to me. She said, "Help me finish what I started."

Mrs. Reddick, today, I am honoring you because today the mission has been accomplished. We have a chief diversity officer that will be paying attention to both sides of the house. You heard Superintendent Eakins describe the passion behind it. I think that based on the conversation that we had; you see that this mission has been accomplished. I honor you today and bring you flowers to be able to solidify this mission.

Since, if I'm not mistaken, you took on this battle in 2001 to create the Office of Supplier Diversity. Mrs. Reddick this is for you today. I honor you. [Flowers were presented with a standing ovation]

Kenneth: Speech!

Doreatha Edgecomb: While the chair is making a presentation, I could not let this moment pass because as I listened to the introduction of the principal of Lockhart Elementary, it took me back to the days when Mrs. Reddick was my fifth-grade teacher. So, as she recognizes you, I want to thank you personally for always setting the bar high for all of us with fifth-grade status. For continuing to be in this community and someone who we would want to emulate.

Personally, I want to thank you for always being the person that I could often go to for encouragement, motivation and helping us make the right decisions.

Thank you for the wonderful fifth-grade year, such that I could start to take your place. And thank you for having divine wisdom. It is an honor and privilege to have you in my life and that I could walk in a path behind you to where I am today.

Susan Valdez: Thank you very much. Mrs. Reddick, if you would like to say few things you can use that mic.

Mrs. Reddick: I can walk a little, but I am so filled with excitement that I'm afraid that if I walk, I might faint.

I have not met the superintendent personally, [turning to address him directly] but I've seen you on TV, and I'm very proud of you and love that you are going to do the right thing to carry this group, this city, and this state forward.

I had Doretha as a little girl when she was about nine years old or so. She was a wonderful person, and she still is.

She was a little girl I admired. Doretha I am so proud of you, so very proud of you. However, she was the one who walked around saying "I'm going to be just like you, Mrs. Perry", and I declare she did.

I worked diligently as I became a school board member. It really was not my choice. It was the choice of a group of young black men who came to ask Mr. Reddick if he would run for school board membership because Reverend Lowry was leaving.

He said, "No, I'm a bit too old. If you had asked me this 10 or 15 years ago, even though they were not offering these things to people of my color, I would have been glad to do it."

The young guys said, "Well if you don't do it, she will have to."

I was disgusted with that because my son was one of those guys in that group. Later he came and asked me when we were having a meeting with my mother in her room. My mother, Clemmie James, was very sick.

I said, "What do you think Mother?" and she said, "Go For it!" in such a demanding way even though she was sick that I said, "You too!" I had so much help from so many people in Hillsborough County; I had to put forth as much effort to win as possible.

I want to thank my children for their support during those years; I don't know if I ever did. But it's just been a marvelous experience, and what I saw today, I like.

I like your organizational chart; your explanation and it was all very clear. Now the next thing is to put it into action. I am sure that as I sat here and looked at you all, I had a good seat. I looked at everybody. I looked into your eyes, and I know what you are going to do because my son tells me all the time that "Your eyes tell me what you are going to do before you say anything. I see it in your eyes." As I was sitting here looking in your eyes, I was seeing what you are going to do.

I'm soon to be 89 years old, but I'm going to be around. So, if you need me, I will be here, and I have broad shoulders.

You look so prosperous and with such plans, this is a new day, a team and a new forward march. I want you to go forth and do what you have to do to make that chart a reality, OK? If you don't, young man, you are going to see me around!!

Thank you so much.

That's my daughter Clemmie, a curriculum development specialist. That's my son Ross who is a computer geek. If you need some computer work done, give him a call. We all run the business so give him a call.

Susan Valdez: "Ross, stand up to be recognized."

Mrs. Reddick: This one behind me went back to the school system after he retired. He said, "You know mama we all carry AARP cards."

Oh, the person sitting next to him is my historian, and I'm writing a book. Listen out for when my book is going to be announced. You are going to appreciate that.

Thanks again for everything. Thank you so much for inviting me here today.

Someone shared a laugh with Kenneth and said, "You think anybody is going to take the mic from her?" They both agreed. No.

Mrs. Reddick:

Susan, keep up the good work, OK? Call me now. I could use a telephone call now and then.

Thank you all.

Doretha Edgecomb & Doris Reddick

L - R: Henry Ballard, Ben Moore, Susan Valdez, Lewis Brinson, Doris Ross Reddick

President Bill Clinton & Doris Ross Reddick

Geraldine Twine, Chantel Copeland, Norene Copeland, Doris Ross Reddick, and Dorothy Height at the NCNW Conference in Daytona, FL

Earl Lennard, Chloe Coney, Doris Ross Reddick, Clemmie Perry

Sam Gibbons, Pat Frank, Delia Sanchez, Doris Ross Reddick

Bold Board Moments

As I shared information about my life for this publication, I wanted to focus on family because my time on the Board came with tough emotional moments. Some of these moments I choose not to remember because I always did what I thought was fair and right. Everyone didn't agree, and some people were saddened by some decisions. However, I am proud of never compromising my beliefs. It is well documented that I was "the lone black member" of the Board and I was indeed determined to make a difference.

Integration:
A few young black students here and there were distributed throughout the county, but we were not fully integrated from the beginning. All administration had done was pick the more talented black students and sent them to white schools. I made it known every chance I got to include more blacks at the administrative level, school level, and when determining student placement.

Judge Elizabeth A. Kavachevich, a federal judge, was in Tampa to determine whether the Hillsborough County schools were integrated and no longer needed federal protection. I testified "No."

After the lawyers, Attorney Warren Dawson of the NAACP Legal Defense Fund and Attorney Tom Gonzalez of the Hillsborough County School Board, questioned me the judge said, "May I ask you a question [as the lone black school board member]?" I said, "Yes you may." She asked if I thought the schools had reached the point of not needing federal protection. I told her, "No, I don't believe they have, and I don't think they ever will. "

Some of my fellow Board members said, "That's a very hot seat, isn't it?" I responded, "No, I just told them what I think." Even against popular opinion, I spoke truth.

In fact, today as I see it, and according to discussions with parents about teachers, they seemed to be re-segregating black teachers and students.

When they looked like me:
A black teacher, who used illegal drugs, was brought before the Board and given a couple of chances to get her life back on track. When she returned, she tested positive again. She offered many excuses including taking cold medicine. I didn't believe her and voted for her to be let go. It was the only fair thing to do. That's how I saw it and I also found it telling that she did not allow anyone of her immediate family or close friends into the hearing. A fellow school Board member advised me that when it is apparent your true stance on an issue is a losing one, you can go another way. I never participated in that. I called it as I saw it.

Blue Collar Workers:
Several men were accused of gambling during working hours and were fired. They were a multi-cultural group of about seven or eight men who were white, black, and Hispanic. A representative of the group told me about their situation. Because of playing penny games during their break or lunchtime, a first-time home buyer was going to lose his home, and college would stop for another child.

I knew of many white officials who were accused of behavior very unbecoming of a person in our profession who received a position change, workplace change or a slap on the hand and nothing else.

I made a comparison and brought it to the attention of Superintendent Sickles.

The men lost their positions. However, they were eventually allowed to return to their jobs and went on to be model employees.

Saving a Key Program
ATOSS (Alternative To Out of School Suspensions) was

one of my pet projects. At one point, it was in danger of not being funded. In fact, we were preparing for a vote to cut the program. I couldn't sit there and let the program go without a fight, so I deferred the vote. This move saved the program. I was so happy when the School District looked at the program again and decided to keep it.

It filled a great need for students. They were not subjected to a perpetually downward process of being suspended from school, losing time in school, falling behind in studies and possibly getting into criminal behavior when forced to stay home alone. ATOSS began with the District's work with HOPE, the Hillsborough Organization for Progressive Equality.

Honoring Our Heritage

Governor Jeb Bush appointed me to the African American History Task Force. The Florida Legislature created the task force to ensure that Florida students are taught about the struggles, triumphs, and contributions of blacks in the United States. I have always advocated for Black History to be taught in the school system, so I was delighted with this assignment.

Quiet Force

On October 21, 2004, The St. Petersburg Times reported in an article about two principals being transferred, "School Board member Doris Ross Reddick, whose late mother is the namesake for James Elementary School, has been publicly critical of the various problems at Washington and James. After she had voiced her concerns, administrators began scrambling to improve conditions such as overflowing toilets and libraries without books at the schools."

Four years earlier on October 08, 2000, Sarah Schweitzer of the St. Petersburg Times wrote about what she called "pure Reddick." She defined my style as, "Her words were measured, chosen with the care of a bride picking a wedding gown; her tone restrained and modulated; her criticism plaited with praise. Her smile is disarming." Indeed, I am a listener and do not bang on desks. I usually apply a little bit of sugar with any castor oil I hand out. This is a method that has worked well for me even though I have been criticized for being too quiet. I operated within the reality of my surroundings. Candy Olsen, another school board member who was quoted in the same article, spoke the truth when she said, "We are much more able to hear and respect what she says because she puts it in such a gentle and clear way." In other words, they would not have heard a word I said if I had screamed at them.

Kenneth says that the word is out there about how soft spoken I was but, if you were on the other side of the table when I was on a mission or angry, you might not think I was so soft. He said it just meant that I operated with the precision of a surgeon and it may have taken you some time to feel the pain.

There truly were days when I was not sooo quiet. One such was when I attended a state school board meeting in Polk County. I traveled with Mrs. Marian Rogers because we were fellow school board members, and our children went to the same schools, Plant, and Wilson.

All was well until the last meeting that dealt with desegregation and the black person experience. The discussion continued during breakfast. Mrs. Rogers disputed something that was said, and I replied, "That's not true!" She said, "It is true! I'll ask my children."

I slide across the top of the table and in her face to make my point. How dare she imply her children's experience carried more weight than mine? I was so mad I had to leave and get some ice cream to cool myself down. I stopped by the Jacksonville table and talked to them for a bit. While I was gone, Rogers asked the Hillsborough people why I was acting that way. They told her because she was wrong.

The next morning, after talking to Harold, I went to the

meeting a little early. I sat with another group and waited for my group to arrive. When they came in, I joined them and sat right next to Marian. Everyone was pleased with that. I had decided I was not going to let anyone, for any reason, make me change from being a nice person.

Other School Board Milestones:

During my time on the Board, I was truly pleased that Blake and Middleton High Schools were rebuilt using black architects. Cheikh Sylla was the architect for Middleton and Harry Howard for Blake. I am emotionally tied to both schools. I attended Middleton, my oldest son went to Blake, and it was built on the site of the historic Clara Frye Hospital. All three of my children were born in Clara Frye. For me, it is kind of sacred ground.

August 17, 2004 was my last day as a school board member and my last act was a letter thanking Dr. Earl Lennard. I wrote:

> *"I want you to know that my family and I are extremely pleased with the outstanding fashion my retirement reception was carried out..........I am getting a much-needed rest after so many years of sharing my life as a servant of the people; however, I really miss you and our conferences in our efforts to leave no child behind. If I can ever be of assistance to you, please let me know. I still have a little more standing room on my shoulders."*

Leaving the Board

After twelve years of service, over three terms, I decided that was enough.

These were my closing remarks as reported in the St. Petersburg Times on November 16, 2004, by Melanie Ave:

> Carver Exceptional Center will keep its name when it moves next year. The center is named after George Washington Carver, a celebrated African American botanist, and inventor who was the son of a Missouri slave.
>
> "I think it is important for children to know people like George Washington Carver," Reddick told fellow board members.
>
> She explained how Carver was "one of the greatest scientists ever known." She peered through her glasses and ended her remarks with a characteristic question, "Okay?"
>
> She stood up for issues affecting black children, employees, and contractors. She said, "I bubbled over when outstanding African-American students came before the board to be recognized."
>
> The only black member of the board, Reddick cast the lone dissenting vote when the board four years ago approved the choice plan - which I call the "chance plan" - that replaced busing for desegregation this fall.
>
> Reddick raised concerns this year about equipment delays and crowded conditions at Booker T. Washington K-8 School and Clemmie Ross James K-8 School, which is named for her mother, who was a teacher. Most of the children at the two schools are black. After Reddick's comments, administrators hustled to improve the schools. Reddick worried about children going door-to-door [to collect donations for their school].
>
> The procedures were altered. For safety reasons, school children are now forbidden from going to people's homes to raise funds. Reddick's spot on the board will be filled by retired educator Doretha Edgecomb, one of her former students, who becomes the board's only black member.

My Spiritual Experience

For my first outing as a baby, Mother took me to a "sanctified" church just down the street from our house. Even though the family was mainly A.M.E. (African Methodist Episcopal) due to my grandfather being an A.M.E. Minister, Mother wanted to go to the "sanctified" church that was near home. I had been christened in the old Allen Temple A.M.E. Church on Scott Street.

I have always been interested in different faiths and studied those that impressed me. The Bahia Faith was one that interested me. For them, it only took nine people to have a spiritual service. They were just fine with meeting in someone's home; a big church building was not a requirement. It was around 1952 or 1953 when I first heard of them from one of Mother's friends. Mother and I accepted her friend's invitation to meet with them. I remember that educated people spoke and they had a big spread of healthy food. They strongly believed in God, but that Jesus was a follower and not the son (I couldn't accept that). Requiring followers to learn the Persian language didn't help the cause either. One of the world-renowned boxer Joe Lewis' sisters, Ms. Barrow, came to Tampa on a recruiting trip, and Mother's friend really pressured us to join. She was unsuccessful, but there was one life changing moment where I heard a featured speaker, and professor from Livingston College say, "A black person is to the Bahia Faith as the pupil is to a person's eye." That, I liked.

Mother's church was Allen Temple A.M.E. She met my father at St. Paul A.M.E. and Mr. James at Allen Temple. Grandmother Hattie went to Mt. Olive A.M.E. because it was close. Uncle James Jones, Aunt Ethel's husband, was an A.M.E. pastor and presiding elder when the current 34th Street Mt. Carmel A.M.E. building was constructed. His name is on the cornerstone.

At Bethune-Cookman, we were required to attend Stewart Memorial United Methodist, at least one Sunday per month. We could attend other churches the other Sundays. Some friends and I decided to join the Episcopal Church and participated in the confirmation ceremony. We wore white dresses and veils. I didn't like drinking out of the same cup, though.

Back in Tampa, I went to Allen Temple with Mother, visited Aunt Ethel as the first lady of Mt. Carmel and at times went to an Episcopal Church. I joined Bethel A.M.E. on Laurel because it was close.

All of the churches to this point were black churches. When I married Harold, he was a member of St. Paul United Methodist Church where the congregation was a mix of black, Hispanic and white people. I went with him and, at times, I visited Beulah Baptist.

When my husband Harold Reddick and I joined Hyde Park United Methodist Church, we were the congregation's first black couples. We joined the church, which was five minutes from our house after our Ybor City church closed.

I settled at St. Paul United Methodist with Harold. Harold and others were having meetings in the 22nd Street area where people needed help. They realized there was a need for a religious component to what they were doing. They talked to Pastor Nevis, who was Hispanic, and asked if they could use his church. Pastor Nevis responded with, "Come on and worship with us. Let's combine efforts." Years later the congregation's membership declined, and the church closed. The monies could not support the required pastor's salary and other church needs. However, some donated funds allowed them to maintain a Roa's Ark program. Harold and I were very active with that effort. When the church closed, the membership went to Christ United Methodist which was mostly black. Because Harold wanted to go to an integrated church, we visited several churches. We found Hyde Park United Methodist and decided to join; we became the pupil in the Hype Park United Methodists' eye. It was a very good move. We traveled and represented the church on many occasions. Harold was elected to one position after the other, and he was happy to serve. It was fun.

Over time, we were often asked, "How did you decide to come here?" Our response became, "God sent us." The typical response was, "You couldn't get here a better way."

With all being said, I firmly believe it was only through the grace of God that any of what I have done and experienced was possible. Supporting me in my spiritual journey were Allen Temple A.M.E., Mt Olive A.M.E., St. Paul United Methodist Church and Hyde Park United Methodist Church.

Doris Ross Reddick speaking to students

Words That Linger

Doris Ross Reddick Quotes

On Children and Schooling
- "We need a strong early childhood education component to build a solid foundation."
- "We need more flexibility in our tracking system so that those who need more stimuli can move up and those who become overly challenged can have a chance to be successful."
- "Our schools need a non-biased history curriculum including all ethnic groups"
- "Our schools must respect the uniqueness and individuality of each child."
- "We must view the home as an extension of our educational grounds and provide parents with the information they need to rear responsible children."
- "All children should be given the opportunity for mobility in society. We must prepare them to cope with change."
- "We need increased cooperation between the schools, government and the private sector to give our children the skills they will need in the workplace."

On Life
"We cannot change yesterday that is clear,
Or begin with tomorrow before it is here,
So, all that is left for you and for me,
Is to make today as good as it can be."

On Her Character
- "I'm a listener. I don't bang on desks."
- "My independence is a strength and not a weakness"

From Speeches:

☐ To 1996 USF black freshmen students: "Young men and women you are black pearls. You are like crown jewels.... You twinkle, you shine, you reflect the world around you, and you have great value. You are jewels to be treasured, jewels to be polished, jewels to be protected and jewels that will increase in value for many years to come."

"You are here to further the tradition of greatness. I want you to know that men and women of greatness have shared common values on education. They decided that their paths would be paved with faith in the Supreme Being & in themselves, sound principles, a sound mind, and a sound education. These things added up to Identity, Ingenuity, and Integrity." .... "We kept our I's on the prize."

☐ To a graduating class: "Each experience you encounter is a learning experience and the more you learn, the more you earn."

"You must protect yourself against negative influences whether of your own making or as the result of negative people. Be a positive thinker."

"People who have accepted themselves as failures will find ways to fail. Those who accept themselves as winners and work toward that end will certainly achieve positive results."

"When there is nothing around us that speaks of salvation, we find it within the knowledge that we are not alone. The God of our forefathers is a guiding spirit as we face the struggles of life."

[Excerpts from what appears to have been a high school graduation speech]:

"Who Are We? We are a Very Special People!"
Like James Forten, the businessmen, abolitionist and advocate for women's voting rights, we are lovers of liberty. We are people who have defended the freedom not only of the United States but the world.

Our blood has been shed in the Revolutionary War, the Spanish-American War, the First and Second World Wars, Korea, Vietnam, and the Persian Gulf. We have never failed to answer the call to defend the United States of America, the nation that is our home."

"Who are we? We are people of distinction!"
Like Lewis H. Latimer the artist, poet, draftsman and inventor who among other things worked on patent applications, including those of Alexander Graham Bell, the inventor of the telephone."

Like Ida B. Wells, the teacher, writer, and organizer who spoke out against injustices."

As did the author of "Crusader Without Violence," the first biography of Martin Luther King. L. D. Reddick, my brother-in-law, scholar, historian and activist who not only exposed deplorable situations factually but also pointed out nonviolent solutions."

"Who Are We? We are eloquent people!"
Like Thurgood Marshall, the late great Supreme Court justice, we have prepared ourselves well and have been profound in our understanding and our presentation of the law. As a young attorney, Thurgood Marshall came to Tampa, Florida in the early forties. He served as a member of the NAACP Legal Defense Fund as legal counsel in the case of our

own beloved Hilda T. Turner, an African American Teacher at Middleton St. High School. Turner served as plaintiff in the successful class action suit against the Hillsborough County School District for equal salaries for black teachers.

"Who Are We? We are trailblazers!"

"Like Olive Florene, my dear cousin, Spanish teacher, guidance counselor, and one of the founders of the Young Adults for Progressive Action, an organization with its primary goal to improve the political, educational, and economic conditions of African Americans in the Hillsborough County community. Florene was one the first two black persons to enroll at the University of South Florida, the other being Hazel Phillips. They were in the summer sessions as part-time students; they were there in the segregated institution testing the climate for the entrance of the thousands of African American students and teachers who were to follow them."

"Who are we? We are courageous people!"

Like Martin Luther King, who saw the mountain top!

Like Rosa Parks who refused to accept any longer the unconstitutional laws of segregation on public transportation.

Like E.D. Nixon, who posted bond for Rosa Parks' release from jail.

Like A. Phillip Randolph, with his melodious voice and courageous spirit, who persuaded President Franklin D. Roosevelt to issue Executive Order 8802 – which banned discriminatory practices in defense plans.

Like Malcolm X who grew impatient with promises and weary with waiting for the love he sent out to be returned."

"Who are we? We are people who think big!"

Like Ben Carson, the young black doctor born and reared in poverty by his sickly mother. Dr. Carson served as the lead physician in separating Siamese twins who were joined at the base of their heads. This was the first operation of its kind in the world in which both children survived and can live independent lives."

"Now who are you, young people? You [pause] are our most valuable assets!
You are young African Americans. You are the descendants of a long line of very special people, artistic people, people of distinction, eloquent people, trailblazers, courageous people, and people who THINK BIG!

You are beginning another adventure in your lives. You will continue your journey in an ever-changing world on technical, informational super-highways that are not yet known. You have great potential. The possibility is within you to develop new discoveries in all walks of life. You can do anything any other group can do if you visualize it and work toward accomplishment as did those who came before you. You are destined to help make this world a better place than you found it. You will carry the torch that you have inherited because you are truly beautiful African American citizens, and you will always be somebody exceedingly special.

I challenge you with the essence of the last few lines Maya Angelou wrote in her poem, And I Rise:

Bearing the gifts our forefathers gone
My beloved young African Americans
Are the hopes and dreams of the slaves
You can rise, you will rise,
It is your responsibility
to rise and still,
You must rise

Again, I congratulate you, we love you, and may God bless you and your families, and do have a great life! The world is waiting for you.

☐ Welcoming a new pastor: "Some individual's' attitudes may be weak, vacillating, fearful or negative. However, as Christians, brothers, and sisters our attitudes must be positive, constructive, assuring and powerful."

☐ To an adult education graduation class: "If you can dream, and struggle and keep going when lesser persons give in... you will have learned the art of living."

Conclusion - Having a Perpetual Impact

My hope is that something from your review of this part of my life has a positive effect, large or small, and be an inspiration that moves you closer to realizing your dreams. My hope is to inspire you to make a difference in at least one person's life. Your impact on others just may show up 100 years later in the life of a president, teacher, trailblazer, parent or simply a productive citizen.

As for me, I will continue trying to make each new day a day to celebrate life. Therefore, my journey is not yet done, and I will share the rest of the story in my next book.

By now you may have wondered, how and why did the seven-year-old Clemmie Simmons predict the future? Well, her teacher was so nice and compassionate she wanted to be like her in every way. Her teacher had a daughter named Doris.

At the end of my mother's life, I asked, "Mother, are you satisfied with your prediction? I am Doris, and I became the teacher you dreamed of." With all the energy my mother could summon, she replied, "More than!"

So, there you have it, "One Person Can Make a Difference!" You can too, so says the Doris Ross Reddick Elementary School song:

We Are The Rays!
We Are The Rays... RAYS of hope!
We're shining stars
We're Reddick Rays
Making a difference near and far
So.....here we come
RAISING the bar is what we're doing.
Here, here we are.
Nothing can stop us now.
Ready to learn more than we know
At Reddick we smile and we shine as we grow
Always above and beyond here we go
We are the RAYS!
We are ready to learn more than we know
At Reddick we smile and we shine as we grow
Always above and beyond here we go
WE ARE THE RAYS

Career Summary

Doris Ross Reddick began her teaching career as a substitute teacher at Simmons Elementary, one of the Strawberry Schools of Plant City, in 1947 and later as a full-time teacher at Dunbar, Meacham, and College Hill Elementary Schools. She integrated George Washington Elementary in the Kingston New York public school system by becoming the first black teacher at that school. Upon returning to Tampa, she rejoined the Hillsborough County School System as a resource teacher. After two years, she served as a Reading Specialist at Carver Elementary. She later became the first Black Learning Specialist/Assistant Principal in the county working at Thonotosassa Elementary School. She was appointed an Educational Diagnostician with the Model Cities Educational Component of the County System and later a Curriculum Coordinator for Early Childhood Learning Centers. Also during her career, she taught adult evening classes at Blake; lectured at Hillsborough Community College and USF, was a USF Criminal Justice Department special research project interviewer; trained Head Start teachers and was a member of the planning team for the first Hillsborough County public school Head Start and kindergarten programs.

She co-authored the language communication study, "Let's Cross Over the Wall" with Mrs. Altamese Simmons to bridge the gap between white teachers and their students during integration. Mrs. Simmons was a former Jackson Heights Elementary principal and very dear friend.

Mrs. Reddick also co-authored "Introduction to Word Processing – Using Theology to Teach Technology" with her daughter, Clemmie C. Perry. This publication is a Bible based approach introducing technology by highlight-

Dr King Drum Major Award Honorees pictured are: Doris L Killian, E. J. Salcines., Chris Turner, James L Ferman, Jr., Rev. John Green, Manuel Alvarez, Donna Parrino, Bernice L Nelson, Doris Ross Reddick, Linnell L.DuPree, Ann R. Porter, and Perry C Harvey Jr.

Doris Ross Reddick
Summary & Reference

YEAR	ORGANIZATION	AWARD
1969	USF EPDA Institue in Standard English as a Second Dialect	Picked from 200 competing applicants
	State of FL Dept of Education	Service on the Advisory Committee for Social Services Technology
1972	Delta Kappa Gamma	Membership
1974	NAACP	Outstanding Service
1987	Community Action of Hillsborough County Special Projects Unit	Outstanding Civic Service
1989	The Early Childhood Learning Center Staff	Dedicated Service
1991	St Paul United Methodist	Roa's Ark
1994	NAACP	Life Membership
1994	Tampa-Hillsborough Urban league	Service to their Drug & Violence Destroy Dreams Program
1995	Middleton High School	Celebrity Basketball Game
1995	Tampa/Hillsborough Dr. MLK Jr commemoration Committee	The Dr. King Drum Major Award for Human Rights & Meritorious Leadership in Keeping the Dream Alive
1995	Hillsborough County Public Schools	Being Elected the First Black Female Chairman of the SBHC
1996	B. T. Washington Jr. High School	Appreciation of Service
1996	YWCA	Tribute To Women & Corporations In Tampa - Education
1997	Don Thompson & H. W Blake High School	Dedicated Service
1998	Tampa Bay Muslim Alliance	Dedication While On The Hillsborough County School Board
1998	Bible-Based Fellowship Church	Serving "Jumpstart 1998-99" parents and students
2002	Hillsborough County	1st African American Female School Board Member
2004	Ladies Of Distinction	Distinctive fortitude & untiring services rendered for the education of children & adults in our community
2004	NCNW	Appreciation – Years of Service – Education Committe
2004	Office Of Govenor Jeb Bush	

YEAR	ORGANIZATION	AWARD
2006	Zonta International	First Ladies of Education in Hillsborough County
2009	Hillsborough County School Board	Doris Ross Reddick Elementary School dedicated
	Tampa Bay Police Dept	Outstanding Achievement in a Traditionally Male Dominated Role
2014	The Buffalo Soldiers	Outstanding Accomplishments
2015	The David C. Anchin Center of the USF College of Education	Dean's Lifetime Achievement Alumni Award

Reference - Doris Ross Reddick Chronicles

For future reference, I am including some of the known news articles and events of my life and family:

DATE		TYPE	SOURCE	TITLE
1845	15-Oct		DR Reddick	Great G Mother - Jane Sherman born
18xx	3-Nov		DR Reddick	Clemmie Simmons James was born
	9-Nov		DR Reddick	Grandmother Hattie Sherman Simmons' birthday
1901	4-Apr		DR Reddick	Charles Samuel Perry was born
1927	13-Mar		DR Reddick	Doris Ross was born
1943			DR Reddick	Graduated from Middleton High
1947	26-May		DR Reddick	Graduated from Bethune Cookman College
1947			DR Reddick	First Job at Dunbar Elementary
1948	June		DR Reddick	Married Charles Perry on Green Street
1949	15-Oct		DR Reddick	Kenneth Perry was born
1949	Aug		DR Reddick	Purchased Grace street house
1950			DR Reddick	Bomb thrown into the back of her house
1955	May		DR Reddick	Went to Mary McLeod Bethune's funeral
1956	16-Oct		DR Reddick	Ross Perry was born
1957	7-Dec		DR Reddick	Clemmie Perry was born
				1st baby born in Tampa Negro/Clara Frye
1961	14-May	Letter	DR Reddick	Mother Darling
1970	22-Aug	News	FL Sentinel	Black Language Barrier- it's real
1974	13-Jul	NEWS	Unknown	Tampians Witness Unveiling of Dr Mary Bethune's Statue
1974			Early History	Big Sisters
1977	16-Aug	NEWS	Community Profile	Deserving of Recognition in Educational Service
1978	20-Oct	NEWS	Division Newsletter	VIP spotlight
1992	2-Oct	NEWS	Tampa Tribune	Reddick Kurdell Win School Posts
1994	1-Feb		DR Reddick	School Board Brochure
1995	17-Jan	SPEECH		SB Awards Ceremony
1995	19-Jun	NEWS	Tampa Tribune	Board May Reschedule Meetings
1995	26-Jun	SPEECH		Summer Graduation
1995	11-Aug	NEWS	Tampa Tribune	Suspended Teacher faces dismissal

DATE		TYPE	SOURCE	TITLE
1995	15-Aug	SPEECH		Black Pearls
1995	28-Nov	NEWS	FL Sentinel	Doris Reddick Elected School Board Chairman
1995	14-Dec	NEWS	DR Reddick	A Lifetime of Lessons
1996	24-Mar	SPEECH		Durrant Dedication
1996	5-Sep			White House Letter
1996	10-Oct	NEWS	Weekly Planet	Class Distinction
1997	9-Aug	NEWS	Challenger	Site Dedication Ceremony - Middleton
1997	10-Aug	BIO	DR Reddick	Celebration of Clemmie Ross James
1998	20-Nov	NEWS	FL Sentinel	Old Williams School Named for Clemmie Ross James
1998	24-Nov	NEWS	FL Sentinel	School Board Must Show Respect for Black Leadership
1998		NEWS	Tampa Tribune	At 71, Integration still her goal
2000	22-Jan	Program	DR Reddick	Health & Ed Assoc Annual Banquet
2000	18-May	SPEECH	DR Reddick	Head Start Celebration
2000	26-Jul	NEWS	DR Reddick	School Notes - Task Force Appointee
2000	26-Jul	NEWS	Carrollwood News	Gov. Jeb Bush appoints to AA History Task Force
2000	12-Nov		Unknown	Sch Deseg Plan Vote 2
2000	15-Nov		Unknown	Sch Deseg Plan Vote 2
2000	15-Nov	NEWS	St Petersburg Times	Board delays vote on school desegregation plan
2000			Highland MB Church	Joined Highland MB Church
2001	2-Oct	NEWS	Times	School segregation case closed
2001	21-Dec	NEWS	FL Sentinel	School Board Rescues ATOSS Program
2001	Sep	NEWS	FL Sentinel	An Educational Banquet
2002	3-Feb	NEWS	Unknown	Minority Contract Oversight Shaken Up
2002	8-Feb	NEWS	FL Sentinel	School District's office of Supply and Diversity
2002	9-Apr	SPEECH		Greetings
2002	28-Apr	NEWS	Tampa Tribune	Schools' Minority Business Outreach Under Microscope
2002	6-Sep	NEWS	FL Sentinel	Elected Officials Urge Citizens to go to the polls
2003	21-Mar	NEWS	FL Sentinel	New High School Dedicated - Middleton

DATE		TYPE	SOURCE	TITLE
2004	7-Sep	NEWS	FL Sentinel	A changing of the Guard on the School Board
2004	9-Sep	NEWS	Tampa Tribune	No Excuse is Good Enough for Chaos at Tampa Schools
2004	10-Sep	NEWS	FL Sentinel	Waiting in the Eye of Storm
2004	22-Nov	NEWS	Tampa Tribune	Reddick's Tenure Made A Difference
2004		NEWS	FL Sentinel	Tenured School Board Member Declines to Seek New Term
2005	22-Apr	NEWS	FL Sentinel	Dedication Ceremony Held for James School
2006	13-Jan	NEWS	FL Sentinel	Tampa Native Returns Home to Accept A Position with Lockheed Martin Corporation
2007	7-Sep	NEWS	La Gaceta	Silhouettes - Doris Ross Reddick
2007	13-Nov	NEWS	FL Sentinel	School Named for 1st Black Woman Board Member
2008	27-Jan	NLTR	DR Reddick	USF
2008			CAL	Calendar Picture and bio
2009	27-Mar	NEWS	FL Sentinel	Women's History Month Event
2010	17-Jan	NEWS	St Petersburg Times	On dialect, hear them out
2010	10-Apr	audio	KEPX Radio	Princess Memories Interview
2010	2-Dec	NEWS	Weekly Challenger	Do What You Can to Make the World A Better Place Than How You Found it
2011	29-Apr	NEWS	FL Sentinel	85th Birthday Celebrated - Mary Alice Dorsett
2011	5-Jul	NEWS	Tampa Tribune	Conditions Bad Bad Bad Bad at 2 Urban Schools
20XX		NEWS	Tampa Tribune	Board Uploads Corporal Punishment
NA		NEWS	Times	More Dollars Go to Minority Firms
NA		NEWS	Unknown	NCNW Members at Guest Night

Reference - Education - Family Legacy

Relationship	Family Member	Achievement
Mother	Clemmie Ross James	Assist Principal & Elem. teacher
Aunt	Ethel M. Jones	1st Dean at Blake High School/Lomax
Cousin	Olive Florene Jones	Spanish teacher
		Middle school counselor
Self	Doris Ross Reddick	Teacher/school board chair
Son	Kenneth Perry	Middle school teacher / coach
Daughter	Clemmie Perry	Corp Training & Documentation
Husband	Charle Perry	Teacher / coach at Blake
Cousin	Alva Simmons (Alphonso's daughter)	Supervisor - ATOS
Aunt	Lorraine Simmons (Alphonso's daughter)	Social worker - HCS teacher
Daughter-in-law	Jessie Perry	Teacher
Cousin	Patty's grandson	PE Supervisor
Cousin	Eddie Mae Ford	Lake Magdalene teacher
Cousin	Sandra McCall	Teacher
Cousin	Jean W. Speedtone	Teacher - NY District
Cousin	Yvonne Speedtone	Teacher
Cousin	Dr. Leroy Kerny	Co-organized a school in Detroit
Cousin	Eliza's grandchild	Teacher
Cousin	Allison Curry Green (Herbert's daughter)	Teacher in California
Uncle	Alphonso Simmons	Teacher

If your name is not here and should be, I apologize. I just wanted you to know you are a part of a wonderful legacy.

I invite you to pick up where I ended, add your name and continue to tell the story.

Index

Africa 38, 87
African American History Task Force 122
A.M.E. 15, 17, 24, 40, 75, 130, 131, 132
   Allen Temple 75, 76, 77, 130, 131, 132
   Bethel 131
   Mount Moriah 17
   Mt. Carmel 130
   Mt. Olive 130
   St. Paul 75, 130
Andrew
   George 9
Angelou, Maya 138
Armwood, Blanche 31
ATOSS 56, 121, 122
Aunt Jemima 96
Bahia Faith 130
Ballard, Henry 113, 114, 119
Bealsville 31, 76
Berry, Frankie 85
Bethune 15, 16, 22, 38, 39, 40, 43, 44, 49, 84, 85, 101, 130, 145
   Mary McLeod 40, 41, 43, 84
Bethune High Rise 101
black dialect 97
Bowden, Rhudine 39, 85
Bush, Jeb 104, 122
Butler, Herbert "Buddy" 25
Calco, Prudy Manis 108
Carson, Ben 104, 138
Carver, George Washington 42, 58, 95, 101, 127
Central Life Insurance 84
Church
   First Baptist 36

Clara Frye Hospital 124
Clarke
   John 76
Cole's Transfer Company 77
College
   Tennessee State 55
   Tuskegee Institute 48
College and Universities
   Tennessee State 55
College & Universities
   Bethune-Cookman 22
   Cornell University 70
   Daytona Industrial School for Girls 15, 40, 43
   Edward Waters 17, 33, 75
   FAMC 17, 33, 75
   FAMU 17, 33, 75
   Hillsborough Coummunity 17, 33, 75
   Rollins 70
   Tuskegee Institute 48, 49
   University of South Florida 48, 49
Copeland, Norene 22, 66, 125, 137
Curry
   Hattie B. 25
   Herbert 25
Curtis Hall 42
Daniel, John 108, 109
Davis, Ed 84
Detroit Gems 48
Doris Ross Reddick Elementary School 142, 146
Edgecomb, Doreatha 116
Edward Waters 17, 33, 75
Elder Hostel 145
Emancipation Proclamation 9, 10, 84
Essrig
   Cecile 20, 21, 22, 100, 101
   Cecile Waterman 20
   Emily 65, 66
   Katherine 21, 22
   Lee 21, 22

Faith Hall 42
FAMU
   Florida Agricultural and Mechanical College 33
Florida Collegians 27
Fordham, Bill 89
Fort Hesterly Armory 89
Freeman, Sandy 55
Fuller, Fred 49
Golden Key Grocery Store 35
Grace Street 27, 28, 29, 30, 51, 52, 88
Greco, Joe 108
Green Street 23, 24, 25, 27, 28, 29, 30, 31, 51, 54, 88
Hamilton, Eva B. 31, 84
Hammond, James A 87
Harris, Harold 95
Hattie 12, 15, 16, 18, 20, 21, 23, 24, 25, 26, 27, 28, 40, 43, 54, 57, 58, 75, 84, 88, 130
Head Start 100, 144
Helping Hand Day Nursery and Kindergarten 54
Hernandez, Maria 85
Hillsborough Community 144
Hillsborough County School Board 20, 22, 63, 81, 105, 106, 112, 116, 120, 145
Howard, Harry 113, 124
Hughes, Langston 42
Hurst, Andrew "Andy" 109
Hurston, Zora Neale 42
Hyde Park United Methodist 131, 132
James
   Clemmie 23, 24, 65, 77, 86, 117
   Clemmie Ross 75
   Clemmie Sherman 78
Jim Crow 88
Johnson, Jack 27
Jones

Florine 51
Olive Florene 87
Jones, Eloise Miller 22
Jones, James 130
Joyner, Marjorie Stewart 42
Kavachevich, Elizabeth A. 120
King
   Adaline 10
   Amanda 10
   Ann 10
   Brack 10
   Clara 10
   Collie 10
   Dora 10
   Eliza 10
   Ezekiel 10
   Joseph 10
   Julia 10
   Martin Luther 87, 89, 136, 137
   Nathaniel 10
   Sophia 10
   Steve 10
   Susan 10
   William 10
Kingston Teacher Association 93
Lang, Doris 85
Legette Drug Store 88
Lennard, Earl 124
Let's Cross Over the Wall 2, 97, 144
Lewis, Alice 49
Lewis, Edgar 49
Lockhart, John W 93
Lowry, A. Leon 87
Maddox, Susie 85
Marshall, Thurgood 85, 136
Martin, Roland 38
May Day 31, 34, 37
Mays Family 9
McKay
   D.B. 20, 26
   Donald Brenham (D.B.) 26
   K.I. 20, 26

Olive 26
Shirley 20, 26
McLeod
   Johnnie Ward 51, 54
   Rudolph 54
Miami Dolphins 62
Miller
   Eloise 22
   Norene Copeland 66
   Pattie B. Sherman 20
Miss Graham 42
Moore
   Annie Mae 44
   Evangeline 44
   Harriett 44
   Harry T. 44
Mrs. Hacker 42
Myles, Derek 112
NAACP 44, 76, 77, 89, 103, 120, 136, 145
NCNW 63, 76, 77, 90, 125, 145
New York 27, 57, 61, 70, 88, 93, 94, 96, 144
Nixon, E. D. 103
Obama, Barack 63
Olsen, Candy 123
Ormond Beach 42
Palatka 15, 25, 75
Parks, Rosa 35
Pastor Nevis 131
Paul United Methodist 131
Pemienta, Americus 85
Perry
   Charles 27, 48, 50, 59, 68
   Clemmie 2, 5, 60, 62, 63, 64, 67, 77, 78, 81, 126, 142, 146
   Ellen 60
   Emily 65, 66, 68, 69, 70
   Jessie Mae McBride 55
   Kenneth 54, 106
   Ross 57, 58, 59, 61, 62, 67, 68
   Ryon 65, 66, 68, 69, 70

Sandra 58
Plant City 48, 49, 76, 92, 93, 144
Pullman Porter 14, 38, 103
Randolph, A. Phillip 103
Reddick
   Harold 6, 65, 66, 70, 74, 87, 95, 100, 101, 103, 106, 123, 131, 145
   Harold II 70
   Jamaica 69, 70, 71
   Naima 69, 70, 71
   Phyllis 70
Ripper, Mary 108
Roa's Ark 66, 101, 102, 131
Robert City Hotel 22, 51
Robinson, Joseph W. J. 110
Rogers, Marian 123
Roosevelt, Eleanor 42
Ross
   James 13, 14, 38, 75
School
   Booker T. Washington 34, 35, 36, 127
   Carver Exceptional Center 127
   Cecile Waterman Elementary 20
   Clemmie Ross James Elementary 122
   Clemmie Ross James K-8 74
   College Hill Elementary 93
   Dunbar 93, 144
   George Washington Carver Elementary 54, 58, 95
   George Washington Elementary 93
   Gorrie Elementary 58
   Howard W Blake High 101, 113, 124, 144
   Jackson Heights Elementary 144
   Lomax Elementary 93
   Lucy Morton Training 39
   Marshall High 50
   McFarland 17, 36
   Meacham Elementary 93

Middleton Senior High 35, 36
Plant High 59
Simmons Elementary 49
Thonotosassa Elementary 95
Schweitzer, Sarah 122
Scott, Thomas 108
Sherman
   Jane 18, 20, 21, 23, 43
   Jim 9
   Pattie B. 20
Sifford, Charlie 63
Simmons
   Alphonso 24, 26, 27, 88
   Altamese 24, 26, 27
   Alva 6, 24, 26, 27, 75, 109
   C.C. 15, 17, 25, 40
   Charles 24, 26, 27
   Ethel 24, 26, 27, 51
   Eva 24, 26, 27, 51
   Hattie 12, 15, 16, 23, 24, 25, 26, 27, 28, 40, 43, 54, 57, 58, 88
   Leola 24, 26, 27
   Pattie 24, 26, 27
Sloan
   Alfred 9
   Andrew 9
   Anita 9
   Charlie 9
   George 9
   Harriett Sherman 9
   Johnny 9
   Matilda 9
   Paul 9, 10
   Paul Jr 9
   Willie Ben 9
Soldier Field 49
St. Paul United Methodist Church 66
St. Petersburg Times 122, 127
Strawberry School 49
Sylla, Cheikh 113 124
Tallahassee 33, 40, 60

Tampa 2, 21, 22, 24, 25, 26, 31, 33, 35, 36, 38, 49, 51, 54, 55, 56, 62, 75, 76, 77, 79, 85, 87, 89, 94, 95, 103, 108, 113, 120, 130, 131, 136, 144, 145, 146
Tampa Bay Buccaneers 62
Tampa Bay Federal Credit Union 55
The New Place 59
Trail Blazers 60
Turner, Hilda 39, 85
University of South Florida 22, 137
Valdez, Susan 116, 118, 119
Waterman
   Cecile 20
   Daisy 20
Wheeler, Lymus Richard 27
White Hall 42
Wilson, Emma 31
Women of Color Golf 63
Worden, Larry 95
YAPA 86, 87
   Young Adults for Progressive Action 86
Ybor City 35, 59, 101, 131

1980 after a full and rewarding career. She and her beloved husband, Harold, immersed themselves in ten years of church humanitarian projects, travel and Elder Hostel lifelong learning. Education, politics, and health were their favorite subjects. She also kept her skills fresh by developing curricula for the St. Paul United Methodist Church "ROA's Arch" program.

Mrs. Reddick's community service activities include membership of Bethune-Cookman College Alumni Association; Community Action Agency Board (CAA); National Council of Negro Women (NCNW); National Association for the Advancement of Colored People (NAACP); and the Tampa Community Players.

School Board Service

In 1992, Reddick was elected to the Hillsborough County School Board becoming the first black woman to hold that position and two years later was unanimously elected as chair, and the first black woman to serve in that capacity. She became the voice for children and minority businesses and under her leadership annual minority business allocations rose from a meager $1,084 to millions. She served three terms totaling twelve years and retired in 2004.

Special Awards/Honors

On May 3, 2009, the Doris Ross Reddick Elementary School was dedicated to honor Mrs. Reddick's service. This was another historical moment, for at that time, she took a legendary seat beside her mother, Clemmie Ross James, for whom a Tampa elementary school is named.

Doris Ross Reddick Elementary School May 3, 2009

www.ingramcontent.com/pod-product-compliance
Lightning Source LLC
Chambersburg PA
CBHW040423100526
44589CB00022B/2812